at Risk

Bringing HOPE to Hurting Teenagers

by Scott Larson

Group

Loveland, Colorado

Acknowledgements

Thanks to Dell Erwin, Amy Simpson, Jim Van Yperen, Matt Brubaker, John Kinsley, and Georgia Mae Bracken for their tireless editing, which made this book so much better than it otherwise would have been. Thanks also to the many young people God has used to teach me and whose stories make up the substance of this book.

Most of all I want to thank my wife, Hanne. Her life personifies all the principles that are contained in these pages, better than anyone else I know.

Note: All the stories in the book are true, but the names of all young people have been changed. Names of adults have not been changed.

AT RISK: BRINGING HOPE TO HURTING TEENAGERS

Copyright © 1999 Scott Larson

Visit our Web site: www.grouppublishing.com

Credits

Editor: Amy Simpson

Creative Development Editor: Jim Kochenburger

Chief Creative Officer: Joani Schultz

Copy Editor: Shirley Michaels

Art Director and Designer: Jean Bruns

Computer Graphic Artist: Pat Miller

Cover Art Director: Jeff A. Storm

Cover Designer: Alan Furst

Cover Photographer: Craig DeMartino

Production Manager: Peggy Naylor

Library of Congress Cataloging-in-Publication Data

Larson, Scott, 1959-

At risk : bringing hope to hurting teens / by Scott Larson. p. cm.

Includes bibliographical references.

ISBN 0-7644-2091-7 (alk. paper)

1. Church work with teenagers. 2. Church work with problem children.

3. Mentoring in church work. I. Title.

BV4447.L36 1999   99-21809

259'.23—dc21   CIP

10 9 8 7 6 5 4 3 2 1   08 07 06 05 04 03 02 01 00 99

Printed in the United States of America.

CONTENTS

INTRODUCTION
by Duffy Robbins

Director of Youth Ministry Program at Eastern College, St. Davids, Pennsylvania

I t was Friday, Memorial Day weekend, May of 1995. The freeways of Los Angeles were choked with holiday travelers hurrying to get to their destinations. Traffic was bumper to bumper on the 405 expressway, thousands of cars zooming by in all four lanes.

It's no wonder no one noticed it there on the side of the road. From a short distance away, and especially at highway speeds, it probably looked more like a dead animal or perhaps a little rag doll that had escaped the grip of a small child in a passing car. Even the California highway patrolman who first noticed the object almost missed it as he passed by in his cruiser—his mind focused more on the turmoil on the highway than on the tiny object *next to it.*

But something about the object caught his attention. The trained eye of the veteran patrolman noticed it just as he was about to pass. *The object was moving!*

Quickly the officer veered to the side of the freeway, put on his caution lights, and ran back along the shoulder only to discover that he was staring into the face of a very young baby boy. It was not only moving, but it was very much alive. Blasted by the gusts from passing cars, the baby appeared to be unharmed, amazingly unfazed, and completely unaware that it was crawling only inches away from almost certain death.

It turns out that the child had crawled away from his baby sitter and managed to make his way from his yard adjacent to the highway the short distance to the shoulder of one of California's busiest expressways. Apparently, the child had been there for a while, crawling on the apron of Interstate 405 while driver after driver sped by, oblivious to the life-and-death drama that was playing out just feet from the path.

It's an amazing story to be sure. But what makes it even more stunning is how hauntingly familiar it sounds. And how vividly it reminds us of the young people in and out of our youth ministries who are standing on the edge of disaster. Many of us are just too busy or too focused to take notice and pull over.

That's one of the reasons I have such respect for Scott and Hanne Larson. They're no less busy than the rest of us. They have many "places to go and people to see." They are just as focused as any other youth workers I know. But they are people whose ministry is marked by a steady eye to the side of the road. They are watching for the young people most of us in youth ministry never notice, the ones who get left along the side of the road until one day their stories take a tragic turn—violence, suicide, family crisis, school dropout, drug overdose, a criminal act—one more teenager unnoticed and unhelped by a society too driven to even pay attention.

It is difficult work. Scott and Hanne Larson are familiar with the real-life struggles of working the shoulders of society's highway. They know all too well the frustrations and risks of working with these kids—lost and lonely because they have been neglected by parents, or they have sort of been dropped out of the mainstream as if they were some sort of litter, or perhaps they have wandered into dangerous places because they did not realize their peril.

That's one of the reasons I found this book so compelling. It has to it a ring of truth and authenticity. It is not the kind of book many of us like to read in youth ministry. For one thing, the title doesn't have a number in it (*Fifty Ideas for Baptism, Forty Discussion Starters Using Water Balloons, Thirty Ways You Can Use a Pez Dispenser To Make the Gospel Come Alive*). It is not an "easy answer" primer that gives us nice, neat solutions. It is not a book of quick strategies and cute ideas we can use *this Sunday night.* Don't get me wrong. We need those kinds of books in youth ministry. (Heck, I've written one or two of them myself!) But we also need books that make us think, books that force us to consider attitudes and approaches, books that make us pull off the youth ministry highway long enough to take a closer look.

I have known Scott Larson for almost fifteen years, and I have watched him and his wife dig deep in a youth ministry culture that often calls us to wide and shallow. They have been doing faithful, substantial youth ministry with kids in prisons and juvenile homes in the New England area for as long as I have known them. They have been faithful at this work, not with a sense of martyrdom or anger that the rest of us seem to be passing by without help, nor with a sense of obligation and begrudged duty. Theirs is a ministry rooted in a passion for Christ and the shepherd's heart that will not rest until someone has gone out to seek for the one lost sheep.

One of my favorite memories is being in their home with some of my youth ministry students from Eastern College and watching as they shared their vision and passion with my students. Beneath the calm voices of two people talking about discipleship in the context of a prison ministry, I heard the voice of warriors, people who recognize that this is a war and who have every intention of being faithful to the fight.

I love exposing my students to people like that. I love being exposed to people like that. I'm thrilled that by reading this book, you will allow yourself to be exposed to that kind of vision and passion. Maybe the fact that you're reading this book means that you *are* someone like that. I hope so.

If you are, what you will find in this book is a very readable, practical, thoughtful guide to doing ministry with "at-risk youth." In the pages of this book, Scott introduces us to Kevin, Tina, Reggie, Cal-Dawg, JayBird, Daryle, and many others (including the fairly well-known Onesimus)—young people Scott and Hanne have come across in more than two decades of ministry and kids whose lives have been changed because Scott and Hanne pulled over long enough to share with them about the cross that changed history.

My prayer is that as you read this book it will give you both the heart and the help you need to better minister to the Kevin and the Onesimus in your own youth ministry, or perhaps at least the vision to see that every day we drive by wonderful opportunities and dire needs—sometimes without even slowing down. If nothing else, maybe this book will remind us all that we need to keep a trained eye and a bowed knee for those young people along the sides of the road.

Thanks, Scott and Hanne, for sharing your life, faith, struggles, and ministry with all of us.

FOREWORD

By Dean Borgman

**Professor of Youth Ministries at Gordon-Conwell
Theological Seminary**

very day in America six children and youth commit suicide, thirteen children and youth are victims of homicide, and 316 children are arrested for violent crimes (according to the Children's Defense Fund).

You hardly can pick up a daily newspaper without reading of the consequences of youth at risk in our society. This morning's paper announced a community's demand for better police protection against unruly teenagers. Police officials were forced to transfer police who weren't aggressive enough in patrolling South Boston and controlling its street kids. Yesterday's Boston Globe carried the final article in an extensive analysis of the school shootings of 1998, "Killing in the Classroom." From February 2 to May 21 the United States witnessed seven violent incidents in its schools, which left twenty-three dead, forty-eight wounded, and countless grieving and emotionally traumatized friends, families, and teachers.

This book is sorely needed. It is written by someone who walks the talk. Scott and his wife, Hanne, have for years gone into prisons, led Bible studies, and followed up youthful commitments—even bringing young felons into their home. Scott is known nationwide and beyond as a dynamic advocate for and speaker about troubled youth. I know the wisdom and depth of his teaching at the graduate level. He communicates passionately about young people.

Scott has developed a tool for measuring human and spiritual development of young people along with suggested strategies for mentoring. You can't be with Scott and Hanne long without sensing three things: They love troubled kids deeply, they are passionate followers of Jesus Christ, and they base their wisdom on the biblical principles and the leading of the Holy Spirit. This foundation and hard effort have seen more than one young convicted murderer through the long road back to productive living—and even through college.

At Risk has the ring of authority in its description of the problem and its suggestions of hope. It takes you into the lives and situations of real persons. It is very readable. Its stories are so captivating you will have to turn back and reflect on each living miracle. The best way to do this may be by asking questions as you read.

How did a nice kid like Kevin get involved with homicide? What was it that attracted Kevin to the good news of Jesus? Why didn't much happen in his life after he decided to follow Jesus? What finally got through to Kevin?

Keep asking honest questions as you read this book. How is it I never realized Onesimus (in the book of Philemon) was really a troubled young person? Why is it we separate the Bible from our ministry, which needs biblical wisdom?"

Fortunately or unfortunately, our society is engaged in great debates about families and parenting. This book cuts through much confusion and brings you needed clarity. You will want to understand how Scott is defining "father" and "mother" and what he means by "fathers and mothers in Christ." Such understanding can bring practical guidelines to all who are concerned about youth at risk. You will read about the absence of father and mother role models in young lives and what kinds of compensations for such loss can be established. A real father (Scott) and mother (Hanne) of their own children and of many they have taken in are behind this book.

You won't want to miss the significant story of how Duane comes to believe God is real. Watch Hanne as she works with girls in Minneapolis and talks with the guys living in their home. Notice how Craig responds when Scott hugs him and says, "You know, Craig, I really love you."

You will recognize the outbursts of kids like Tina, Jesse, and Alex. But you may not have brought together the insights of Erik Erikson and the Apostle Paul in dealing with them. This is an important strength of this book.

No book of this kind can avoid the issue of anger. Where does all this anger come from? How can it be measured, and how can we deal with it?

This book doesn't just motivate; it fulfills its promise of giving you practical guidance in working with young people. The four principles for building a relationship with troubled youth or any teenagers are important for any youth worker. Building a strategy for ministry on the basis of an understanding of evangelism as a process will save many mistakes and much frustration.

Marcus was probably right when he told Scott he didn't need the welfare officer's help. All who work with troubled young people need to know what kind of help is helpful. The key to empowering young people to be all they were meant to be is here for all who take this book seriously.

Don't get the wrong impression that this is a success story or just a positive, no-problem approach to difficult ministry. You may find Scott's vulnerability and confession of failure and discouragement the most valuable part of your reading. To those who are really discouraged or burned out, there is a hopeful message here. With God's help and for kids' sake, make the most of this vital volume.

at
Risk

The
BIG
Picture

CHAPTER 1:
Kevin

Hungry, frightened, and clothed in only his underwear, fourteen-year-old Kevin curled up in a corner of a police-station cell and tried to keep warm. Fear gripped his heart, and thoughts of suicide plagued his mind.

A million questions were swirling around in his head. *How did all this happen? Is it just a bad dream? Will I ever see the light of day again?*

As he faced the possibility of spending the rest of his life in prison, sleep didn't come to Kevin that first night in a jail cell. Instead his mind wandered through the past, trying to understand just how he had gotten to this point.

FAMILY MATTERS

As far as a father was concerned, Kevin had never really had one. Sure, there was a man involved—someone had *fathered* him. But that was altogether different from *having* a father. And while his dad might read about this incident in tomorrow's newspaper, he would have no idea it was his son who was involved.

What would happen to his mother? He kept seeing her anguished face in his mind. He couldn't rid his ears of the sounds of her loud wailing at the police station. He knew she would blame herself. So once again, Kevin would be the strong one, saying, "It's OK, Mom. It's OK. Everything's going to be all right."

Kevin knew that his mother's whole life had been plagued with problems. *One more thing like this just might send her over the edge,* he worried as he began to ponder her own difficult past.

Raised in an alcoholic home, Kevin's mother had been sexually abused by both her father and her grandfather as a young teenager. Distrust and abandonment had marked young Sally's life early on, and so it was no surprise that by age fourteen, she was drinking heavily, and by eighteen she had moved out of the house, never to return.

She was married within a few months, and her life went from bad to worse. Her new husband, Sam, turned out to be even more detestable than her father. The honeymoon was short-lived. Alcohol, cursing, beatings, and rape became the norm in their newly established home. There were frequent calls to the police, both from frightened neighbors and from Sally herself.

Surprisingly, the marriage lasted five years. And in the end it was Sam who eventually left Sally. She was so hurt and devastated that she determined never to marry again, a vow she never broke.

That's why everyone was so shocked when Sally fell for Jack only a few years later. He had just moved to town, and he began frequenting the Lamplighter Bar, where Sally worked. Having just experienced the breakup of his third marriage, Jack was also feeling devastated.

As Sally and Jack began to spend time together, they soon discovered how much they had in common. Sally couldn't remember ever having felt so understood by anyone, and the relationship appeared to hold great promise. He was gentle and a good listener, rare qualities in the men she had encountered. It seemed as if they were meant for each other.

Shortly after they moved in together, though, the newness started to wear off. Old patterns began to surface—his inclination toward abuse and her knack for finding it.

Things got much worse when they learned Sally was pregnant with Kevin. The beatings became more frequent and more severe. On one occasion, Jack choked Sally to the point that she blacked out. Soon after, she left him.

Though Kevin was Sally's only child, he was Jack's tenth. He seemed to display a twinge of guilt that he wouldn't be around for this one either. But even though Jack made an attempt to reconcile the relationship after Kevin was born, it soon became clear that it just wasn't going to work. After five weeks, he left for good.

Who needed him anyway? For Sally, not having a man around was more of a relief than anything. Besides, now she had this precious little boy, someone she could shower all her love on and someone who, for the first time, could reciprocate that love. They were inseparable, and for a while her drinking became more manageable. This period of time was the closest thing to a "normal life" that Sally and Kevin would experience together. She worked full time, hiring girls in the neighborhood to baby-sit.

Then out of the blue, Sally's first husband, Sam, started calling again. At first she rejected every attempt he made to meet, but Sam remembered how to kindle the spark in Sally. "Maybe he really has changed," she reasoned. "And it would be good for Kevin to have a man around." Besides, she was growing weary of working all the time and struggling just to keep food on the table.

Sam moved back in when Kevin was five years old, allowing Sally to quit her job. But it didn't take Sam long to discover that he wasn't fond of having a whiny little kid around the house. That tension precipitated many fights. And while Sam was around only for a short time, the impact of his stay would linger much longer.

Kevin recalled the aftermath of those days: "She told me that he used to rape her a lot. One time she got pregnant, and he said she had to get an abortion because we couldn't afford having another kid around. Like lots of the stuff she'd tell me, I was just too young to understand. I only remember that things really started going downhill after that."

Sally's drinking escalated dramatically. She was unable to find another job, and they were soon evicted from the apartment. With nowhere to turn, Sally had to swallow her pride and do something she had sworn she never would. With Kevin in arm, she made her way to the welfare office. While she was able to qualify for assistance, it would require their moving into the subsidized housing projects.

Feeling like a failure and having lost what little self-respect she had, Sally began drinking in binges. She would shut herself up in the house, sometimes for a week or more at a time, consuming scarcely anything but rum and Cokes.

Meanwhile five-year-old Kevin was scrounging up bottles and cans, exchanging them for soup pouches and cupcakes at the corner store. He would search the house for food stamps so he could buy milk and bread. Though he would often make sandwiches for his mom, begging her to eat, she existed largely on a diet of coffee, cigarettes, and booze.

He remembered the afternoon he came home to the sound of loud wailing in the bedroom. Running into the house, he found Sally under the bed. As he struggled to pull her out, she kept sobbing, "Just come and hold me, Kevin. Just hold me." At age six, he began fearing the day when he might come home and find that his mother had drunk herself to death.

To Sally's credit, she never physically abused Kevin. She truly loved him. That's why she felt so guilty for neglecting him every time she would sober up. Trying to make up for it, she would often say, "You don't have to go to school today, Kev. Let's just the two of us go shopping."

But Kevin liked school. He'd grown accustomed to getting himself ready and going on his own since he was in the first grade. But even school didn't come easy for Kevin. In the first grade, he was diagnosed with attention deficit disorder and a moderate speech impediment. He was put on Ritalin and given special education services. Yet he was so determined that by the eighth grade he had received numerous academic awards. He even graduated from middle school with honors.

Recalling those days, Kevin thought of all the positive memories he had of his middle school principal, Mr. Denson. "He knew my mom and my situation, but he never condemned me. Instead he would just keep tabs on me, and any time I would skip school, he'd call me into his office and talk with me—just like a dad."

But at the same time, Kevin was developing a warped sense of identity. Seeing himself as the "man of the house," he felt the responsibility of being both a provider and protector for his mother.

"I always knew I had to protect mom, not only from herself, but also from the teachers and social workers who would ask me questions and send things home for her to sign. I'd sign her name and make up excuses for why she could never attend the parent meetings. I knew that if people saw how things really were, they'd probably take me away and put me in a foster home."

By age nine, he was doing pretty much whatever he wanted. The kids he hung around with at school were pretty positive, but in the projects he was drawn to an entirely different crowd. Because most kids his own age had curfews, Kevin started staying out late with older kids. At first he wasn't doing anything wrong, just watching and learning. He remembered how good it felt just to be included by the older kids.

But as they say, bad company corrupts good character. When he was ten, Kevin started breaking windows in the neighborhood. By eleven he was stealing car stereos and selling them for fifty to seventy-five dollars, justifying that it was a way to generate much-needed money for himself and his mom. At twelve, he became a lookout for a couple of drug dealers in the projects. He could earn an easy hundred dollars just for keeping watch for a couple hours.

At age twelve, Kevin was finally arrested. The charge was shoplifting. Then a couple of weeks later he was arrested again, this time for damaging property. Sally became concerned. She called her sister to see if they could move in with her for a little while. "He just needs to get out of the projects and get some new positive friends," she reasoned.

The opposite actually happened. Because he didn't know anybody in the new neighborhood or school, Kevin started hanging out with his cousin's fourteen-year-old boyfriend. Two years older, Jimmy became like a big brother to Kevin. He also was a member of a local teenage gang called the SSPs (South Side Posse).

A SUBSTITUTE FAMILY

Eager to prove himself, twelve-year-old Kevin started stealing cars and dealing drugs, turning all the money over to the gang. His loyalty quickly gained him acceptance from the leaders, who at first had been wary of him as an outsider.

Kevin remembered those early days in the gang: "The SSPs had four main leaders. One of them became like a father to me, even though he was only eighteen. He was respected and feared in the neighborhood. I would go to him for advice a lot. He was the one who got me my first gun."

During that winter, tensions were mounting between the South Side Posse and their primary rival, the Overland Street Boys. They threatened each other constantly. The issue had always been turf—specifically, who controlled one particular block that separated the two gang territories. But now that one of the SSP members had been jumped and badly beaten, tempers were raging and the issue had switched to revenge.

On the afternoon of March 12, Kevin remembered how surprised he was to see Hector, one of the leaders of the SSPs, waiting for him outside the school. Because Hector never attended or even hung around school, Kevin knew something was up. Hector had come to ask him to be one of three who would accompany him as he followed home the kid who had jumped their friend. Feeling both honored to be chosen and a bit nervous about what might happen, Kevin reluctantly agreed.

In an empty parking lot, what began as a mere verbal confrontation soon escalated into much more. Not satisfied with his adversary's response to the questions he asked, Hector felt this kid needed to be taught a lesson. A fistfight between the two was all he intended it to be.

About five minutes later, another SSP member, trying to make a name for himself, unexpectedly jumped in, kicked the other kid from behind, and knocked him to the ground. He then surprised everybody by pulling a small pistol from his pocket and firing a shot into the side of the boy who was already on the ground.

Stunned by both the shot and the screaming, Kevin and the others started running across the parking lot. About five seconds later, they heard a second shot. Looking back, Kevin saw the body of the boy lying motionless on the pavement. He kept running.

By the time Kevin got home, he was so frightened and hysterical that his cousin could barely understand him. When the leaders of the SSPs figured out what had happened, they started calling associated gang members who lived in other major cities in an attempt to find a place for the boys to go while the heat was on. Kevin, it was decided, would fly to Dallas first thing in the morning and hang low there until things back home had settled down.

Kevin remembers just going into his bedroom. He felt numb. He had never seen anyone die before. He had never even really hurt anyone before.

What had his life come to? What would happen to him now?

Later that evening the police came and arrested him. They handcuffed him to a door at the station while they went back to get Sally. The detective took his clothes to examine as evidence and put him in a cold cell with nothing but his underwear. That night Kevin confessed to the whole thing. The next morning in court, Kevin and his three friends were charged with murder.

Where Are the Kevins in Your Community?

If you minister to teenagers in a local church, you certainly have encountered Kevins. They have attended your youth ministry functions. There have been Sallys who have gotten to know some of the people in your church. She even may have visited your church. If you minister in the context of a parachurch organization, there's no doubt you've met a few Kevins in your day. Some days it may feel like they're all Kevins.

It doesn't matter whether you minister in an urban, suburban, or rural context. The issues that defined Kevin's life (an absent father, an alcoholic mother, abuse and neglect, negative peers, gang involvement, and the lack of effective outside intervention) have become commonplace for an increasing number of young people. As a result, scores of kids like Kevin have come to be termed "at risk." But just how many at-risk young people are there?

Dean Borgman, professor of youth ministries, says, "In my observations of communities across America, teenagers comprise about 10 percent of the population in most cities. Of the total number of teenagers in any given community, about 20 percent are generally fairly well-adjusted—taking active leadership roles and likely to make it fine without outside intervention; 60 percent are experiencing the typical ups and downs of adolescence, perhaps needing help at times; 15 percent are struggling severely with life-controlling problems and are in need of special outside intervention if they are to develop healthily; and the other 5 percent could be considered very dangerous—either homicidal or suicidal. This group will almost certainly inflict damage to either themselves or others unless appropriate intervention is applied."[1]

According to Borgman, 20 percent of the teenagers in your community—or one out of every five—are at risk and in need of serious intervention in their lives. The National Research Council's Panel on High-Risk Youth paints an even dimmer picture. They say that at least seven million young Americans—roughly 25 *percent* of young people between the ages of ten and seventeen—are at risk of failing to achieve productive adult lives! [2]

DETERMINING IF A YOUNG PERSON IS AT RISK

Environmental Factors

HOME

- Alcoholism and/or illegal drug use
- Physical or sexual abuse
- Harsh or unpredictable behavior patterns
- Extreme neglect: receiving little instruction, love, and discipline as a child
- A young mother
- Either no contact or negative contact with father or mother
- Parent or sibling who has been incarcerated
- Parents with severe marital problems

COMMUNITY

- Poorly functioning school system with high truancy and dropout rates
- Violence or strong bullying/stealing on school grounds
- Shootings and drug trade in the immediate community
- High levels of poverty
- Few jobs available in community
- Few or no youth in the neighborhood who attend church or church programs

PEERS

- Strong pressure to join gangs in the neighborhood
- Peers who have been pronounced delinquent
- Absence of positive peer relationships
- Lack of a positive adult role model
- Membership in a gang or a small group that discusses and plans antisocial behavior

Personal Factors

CHILDHOOD

- Hyperactivity and attention problems
- Persistent lying
- Difficult temperament

ADOLESCENCE

- Smoking and/or drinking before age twelve, using marijuana before age fifteen
- Struggles with depression
- Persistent lying
- Lack of guilt for negative actions
- Lack of empathy for others
- Persistent problems with authority
- Binge drinking or drug abuse
- Sexual activity (more than a couple of experiences) before age thirteen
- Sexual abuse (as a victim or an abuser)
- Deep hurt that has led to self-inflicted damage or talk of suicide
- Inner rage that has led to violent acts
- Preoccupation with violence and with playing violent video games
- Obsession with fantasy games and/or the occult, death, and/or the satanic

Any three factors from the "environmental" list plus three from the "personal" list indicate that a young person is "at risk" of hurting self or others. Five or more from each list indicate "high risk." It should be noted, however, that young people with little going against them can destroy themselves or others. Likewise, youth in terrible internal and external danger can make it by the grace of God and/or the resilience of the human spirit. [3]

Just what determines whether a young person is at risk? There is no scientific formula, but the list on page 16 outlines some external, circumstantial factors that affect kids as well as some internal, personal factors.

What Do We Do With Them?

One thing is for certain. If you're working with youth these days, you're encountering more and more at-risk and high-risk teenagers. So what do we do with them? We can either lament over their presence and hope they won't come back, become frustrated that nothing we try seems to work with them, or see them as a gift from God and commit to trying to reach them.

Because you're reading this book, you've probably taken the third approach. You wouldn't be reading a book like this if your heart hadn't been broken along the way for some of these young people. But what is it that makes these so-called at-risk youth so different from the rest? What motivates them? Why do they respond to things the way they do? How do they tend to view life, God, and anyone who tries to reach them?

Why does it seem that nothing we do with the rest of the youth seems to work with them? How can we reach them more effectively? And what is realistic to expect in return? How much do we dare get involved? What is the best role to play in their lives? These are some of the questions this book will address.

I certainly didn't begin youth work with the intention of focusing on the Kevins of the world. In fact, I saw troubled young people as a frustration and diversion to my real desire, which was to invest my energies in the more gifted youth who possessed real leadership potential, the ones who could change the world.

But, perhaps like you, I just kept encountering more and more troubled youth. And strangely enough, God began breaking my heart for them. In fact, for nearly two decades now I have invested my life almost entirely in working with at-risk youth.

At first I saw them as "the least of these," the ones Jesus described in Matthew 25. I felt convicted, thinking, "Who am I to determine which kids I'll minister to and which ones aren't worth the investment of my time and energy?"

Then as I got to know some of them better, I discovered the rich leadership potential that was sitting latent in so many of them. Most of them just hadn't received the same breaks I had. Would I have turned out any different than they had if I had been raised in the same environment?

Then a strange and unexpected thing began to happen. I started to develop a deep, God-given love for troubled young people. I became more and more drawn to the teenagers that others hurriedly passed by—not because I felt sorry for them, but because I genuinely loved and enjoyed them. I wanted to be with them.

To be sure, these teenagers have given me my greatest disappointments and some of my most exhilarating highs. They have contributed to some of the worst days of my life—and undoubtedly some of the best. I don't think I would have known as much pain or felt as much joy if it weren't for some of the troubled young people I've known. And along the way, they've captured my heart. Perhaps that's because they inhabit the place where God's heart beats also.

Throughout Scripture, God seems to actively seek out at least five distinct types of people: the poor, the sick, the orphans, the widows, and the imprisoned. The troubled teenagers you encounter in your community probably fit into several of these categories. And when your heart becomes broken for those hurting youth who cross your path, you can be sure it's God's heart of compassion you're feeling, that your heart is beating in sync with God's. And he just may be calling you to a deeper level of ministry with hurting young people.

ENDNOTES

1. Dean Borgman, personal interview by Scott Larson, Boston, Massachusetts, August 11, 1998.

2. National Research Council, Panel on High-Risk Youth, *Losing Generations* (National Academy Press, 1995), 5.

3. Chart compiled with input from Dean Borgman of The Center for Youth Studies and Peter Vanacore of Straight Ahead Ministries, October 1998.

CHAPTER 2:
Is There a Way Out?

obody had heard of Kevin before March 12. But suddenly, for several days he was a regular on the six o'clock news and the front page in several newspapers. Though the people in his Massachusetts city hadn't known him before, they certainly were talking about him now. Most were incensed, and rightfully so. Concerned citizens cried out, "What's this world coming to?" "Nobody's safe anymore!" and "We need to send a message to kids that this kind of thing won't be tolerated!"

The district attorney in the case was asking for life sentences for all four boys involved in the shooting. An outraged public echoed "Amen." After all, what could be more just?

Unfortunately, Kevin's life is neither an isolated case nor a sensationalized story. He represents millions of teenagers across America. And while the juvenile detention centers are filled with Kevins, the vast majority of them live much lower profile lives, often within a few miles of each of us. Like Kevin, they remain virtually unknown until something tragic happens and suddenly they're thrust into the center of public discussions.

While the streets of Kevin's neighborhood were lined with churches, he never had actually stepped foot into one—never. While some sent buses into his neighborhood to bring kids to Sunday school, youth group, and vacation Bible school, somehow he always got passed over. To his recollection, he had never met a Christian the whole time he was living in that city. How might his life have been different if he had? What if you had met him when he was eight, ten, or thirteen? What might you have done that could have averted the tragedy that awaited him?

This book is not about three easy steps to successful ministry with troubled teenagers. But it does present a biblical model for effective ministry to even the most damaged and dangerous youth. Does that guarantee success and a radical turnaround? Of course not. But it does impact young people, giving them something significant to hold on to, even if that something lies dormant—not bearing fruit for several years. As Scripture says, our labor in the Lord is never in vain (1 Corinthians 15:58).

Although youth ministry is not specifically mentioned in the Bible, one of the most relevant verses for effective ministry to today's at-risk teenagers was penned by the Apostle Paul in 1 Corinthians 4:15: "For though you might have ten thousand guardians in Christ, you do not have many fathers. Indeed, in Christ Jesus I became your father through the gospel" (New Standard Revised Version). Just as it was clear that I had a greater need for a father than for just another guide, so also do troubled teenagers today.

Research has shown that the single greatest factor influencing character development and emotional stability is the relationship one experiences as a child with both parents.[1] An exhaustive study on juvenile delinquency commissioned by the American Society of Criminology concluded, "Of all the factors we have found as contributing to delinquency, the clearest and most exhaustive evidence concerns the adequacy of parenting."[2]

With more and more young people growing up in the absence of two loving parents, the paradigm for effective ministry has rapidly shifted from a programmatic model to one that is much more relational.

But the nature of the needed relationship is also shifting. The yearning of today's at-risk teenager is for a relationship much more akin to what the Apostle Paul described as a mother or father in Christ rather than just a guide, teacher, or friend. So just what does *a mother or father in Christ* look like?

Onesimus

An intriguing model of this kind of relationship is revealed in Paul's letter to Philemon. Here Paul advocates for Onesimus, a runaway slave, who was wanted for stealing from his master, Philemon.[3] The letter to Philemon provides a practical strategy upon which this book is largely based.

Today's troubled teenagers bear a striking resemblance to Onesimus in many ways. First is their age. Onesimus was probably in his late teens when Paul penned this letter.[4]

Second, because Onesimus was a slave—one of 60 million living in the Roman empire in the middle of the first century[5]—he belonged to the lowest class in the Roman world. Slaves weren't even considered people; instead, they were things. If one was born a slave, it almost certainly meant one would die a slave. It was a class that was nearly impossible to break out of. "Rags to riches" stories didn't exist for slaves. People just didn't move from being slaves to being Roman citizens.

Many of today's at-risk teenagers find themselves in a similar predicament. Society looks down on them. And just as Onesimus and other runaway slaves were branded on their foreheads with the letter F (signifying "fugitive") by a hot iron [6], today's troubled teenagers carry the scars of other people's judgments on them: "slow learner," "troublemaker," "loser," "just like your father."

For the millions of teenagers per year who have run-ins with the law, the "branding" can go even deeper. [7] Today's juvenile offenders live with their criminal records long after their sentences are served. For example, current laws and public pressure have banned many teenage offenders from even attending public high schools and colleges in several states, virtually eliminating their access to the educational services afforded others—even if they do manage to turn their lives around. [8]

Third, Onesimus was on the run. Once caught, his punishment would likely be death. Many high-risk teenagers live in the same hopelessness. From an early age, their lives seem doomed for destruction. Many are convinced they won't live to be twenty-one years of age, and this fear becomes a self-fulfilling prophecy for some.

And finally, somebody intervened in the life of Onesimus. Paul shared the good news of Jesus Christ with Onesimus, and he responded. Then Paul began to do something very risky: He began to advocate for this young man's freedom. The stand he took then was no more popular than it is now.

In A.D. 61, probably just a few months before Paul wrote Philemon on behalf of Onesimus, all of Rome was shocked when the prefect of the city, Pedanius Secundus, was murdered by one of his slaves. As a result, the Roman senate voted to enforce a law that already was on the books. They put to death four hundred of the murderer's fellow-slaves—men, women, and children—even though they were well known to be innocent of the crime. [9] This clearly was not the time nor the place to be advocating for runaway, criminal slaves. Paul did it anyway.

Juvenile crime has grown to become one of the greatest concerns of Americans today. [10] With current trends moving toward mandatory sentencing for juveniles, "three strikes and you're out" legislation, and a growing number of youth being tried in adult court, advocating for young offenders isn't popular today either.

When Paul wrote to Philemon, he risked his own reputation on a thief. He asked his friend to drop all charges against Onesimus, who had stolen from Philemon. If that wasn't enough, Paul then requested that Onesimus be freed from his status as a slave and made a free man. Even more, he requested that Philemon make Onesimus a brother and an equal. This kind of a request was unheard of in first-century Rome. Was a runaway slave really worth the risk?

After all, what if Onesimus was just "playing" Paul? What if he took advantage of Philemon's benevolence and then fell away from the faith completely, as so many do? Worse yet, what if Onesimus "re-offended" against someone else? It would be Paul's reputation that would suffer if Onesimus messed up. Was a runaway slave really worth the risk? Apparently, Paul thought so.

What did Philemon decide to do? What ever became of Onesimus? The Bible doesn't say. We don't know for certain. But Ignatius, the Bishop of Antioch, wrote a letter some fifty years later about a man who seems to fit the description of this runaway slave. Ignatius referred to him as Onesimus, Bishop of Ephesus! [11] Apparently Philemon took a risk and did what Paul had requested. And what happened was even more unlikely than a slave becoming a citizen: That slave went on to lead the church in all of Ephesus.

Today's young people also need advocates if they're going to make it. Not just troubled teenagers, but all youth. They need people like Paul, people who believe in them, people who are willing to stick their necks out for them. And do you know what? Even the most hardened of them can change, every bit as much as Onesimus. Given the right circumstances, at-risk youth can break out of their "class," just as Onesimus broke out of his.

Kevin

One of those kids who broke out was Kevin, the boy described in Chapter 1. The courts had decided to try him as a juvenile, partly because of his young age and partly because he wasn't the shooter in the crime.

The first week Kevin was locked up, he attended a Bible study my wife, Hanne, and I were teaching. A couple of weeks later he made a commitment to Jesus. Even though it was the first time ever Kevin had encountered Christians, he said he felt as if a light bulb had gone on inside him when he heard the message that Jesus had died on a cross for him. He said it was the first time he knew there was a God.

Like many, Kevin didn't grow a whole lot in his faith right away. He would occasionally read his Bible, pray for his mom, and pray that he would get out soon. But after being transferred to another facility, he became more and more committed to Bible study and to following Christ. Those who led the Bible study there were committed to Kevin as well. It was while he was in that juvenile jail that Kevin believes he really repented. He recalls going through a period of several weeks where he would cry nearly every night as he realized how sinful he was, saying, "Why did you die for *me*, Jesus?"

When it was time for him to be released, Kevin didn't have many good options for a place to go. Having heard of the aftercare home we run for teenagers coming out of detention centers, he inquired about it through his caseworker, and eventually he moved in with us.

Kevin ended up living with us for two years. Although his life was anything but free of struggles, he did graduate from high school. From our home he went on to a well-known Christian liberal arts college, where he graduated with a 3.65 grade point average, double-majoring in theology and philosophy. From there he received a full scholarship for law school, with the ultimate goal of helping others like himself, teenagers who can see no way out.

Not everyone becomes an Onesimus or a Kevin. Most don't. But that's not our business. The results are up to God. We never know which ones will become Kevins, given the right people in their lives. They're out there. They're in our juvenile prisons. They're hanging out on our street corners. They live down the street from us. They're in your youth group. How will you reach them? A program won't do it. They need someone to be a mother or father in Christ to them.

This type of ministry isn't very flashy. It's not geared toward big numbers. It's anything but easy. Sometimes it seems to take everything you've got—and more. But it's God's way, and it works. Does it mean you have to have troubled teenagers live with you? No. Onesimus didn't live with Paul, yet Paul was a father to him just the same. Do you have to be a father or mother to every troubled teenager in your program? No, but it may mean recruiting many more adults to be surrogate parents to needy young people in your program.

But before we look more in-depth at what it means to be a father or mother in Christ, let's spend a little time on how to initiate relationships with troubled young people.

Initiating Effective Relationships

One of the difficulties of initiating relationships with teenagers is that they can seem intimidating. They seem to be at the center of our culture. They're the ones who know and embody what's in style in terms of clothing, music, and vocabulary. Adults are often portrayed as "old-fashioned" and "out of touch."

This intimidation only intensifies when it comes to at-risk teenagers. Most of us understand very little of what life is like for them. And because of their myriad of trust issues, they're just as leery about getting to know us. So what steps are necessary to initiate a fruitful relationship?

First, realize that you'll have to be the one to initiate the relationship.

Most teenagers won't do it. You may even need to attempt it several times before it begins to gel. At first teenagers may not even take your invitation to get together seriously because they can't understand why you would be interested in getting to know them. But I have yet to hear of a young person turning down a sincere adult who really wanted to get together with him or her. Teenagers may be a bit apprehensive and nervous, but they'll also be blown away by the notion that you actually want to spend time with them.

Keesha was one of the first girls Hanne started working with in Minneapolis. She certainly wasn't the most flattering girl in the world. On one occasion she even told Hanne, "You know, you're probably the most boring person I've ever met." She wasn't a girl you would call if you needed to be cheered up. But Keesha never once turned Hanne down when she asked her if she wanted to get together to talk.

Second, when you're thinking about getting together (particularly with boys), plan the time around an activity. It can be very intimidating for both of you just to get together "to talk," especially if you both realize after about five minutes that you've run out of things to talk about. It may quickly become clear that you don't have much in common, and each of you will wonder, "Now what do we do?"

It's much better if you can organize your time around attending a sporting event, going mountain biking, going to a movie, or getting something to eat. Doing activities together also gives you the opportunity to create memories, things you can talk about again and again in the future. Besides, it's much easier to recruit men to do a specific task, such as coaching, tutoring, or job training, than to just hang out and "bond" with a young person. It's in this process of doing an activity that significant relationships are formed, but that comes as a byproduct.

While this is almost always true for men and boys, it can be different for girls. Girls are much more likely to be open and to want to get together and talk. Girls usually are in touch with their need to express themselves and be heard. Hanne found that she never had a girl refuse to get together with her or any of her female volunteers just to talk. While they ran weekly activities for groups of girls, they were far more excited about the one-to-one interactions.

Third, try to schedule some activities for just the two of you, away from the teenagers' friends. Young people usually act differently when they're with their friends: They have an image to maintain. Never force them to choose between you and their friends, or you'll lose every time. When they're away from friends, though, they can afford to be more themselves.

When you're alone with teenagers, you can talk more about spiritual matters, too. I've found that most troubled teenagers are actually far more open to this than teenagers in general. They usually are more in touch with their needs, and often they haven't been so overexposed to Christianity that they've become bored with it.

Hanne used to do one-on-one Bible studies with girls at the McDonald's in their neighborhood. Their friends were always interrupting, asking what they were doing. They'd proudly respond, "We're having a Bible study," not at all embarrassed.

Fourth, don't be afraid to go on their turf. When Hanne felt called to begin ministering with troubled girls in South Minneapolis, she had only one problem: She didn't know any such girls in South Minneapolis. Her Youth Guidance supervisor recommended that she go to a junior high school and just hang out. That sounded about as appealing to her as spending the afternoon at the dentist's office.

But she did it anyway. When she asked the school principal if she could just hang out in the cafeteria during lunch, the response was different from one you might receive at a suburban school: "Sure, the more adult bodies in here the better!"

When she entered the cafeteria, she understood the principal's enthusiasm. It was out of control. Kids were yelling and jumping on tables. It was no wonder that all the doors were locked during each lunch shift in an attempt to contain the chaos.

Hanne felt scared and intimidated. But she found a table where a girl was sitting by herself, and she sat down to talk with her. They had a good talk, and Hanne kept going back. Eventually she got to know more and more girls there. That group of girls became the core of her ministry for the next several years.

What did they talk about? Well, Hanne realized she didn't know much about what these girls' lives consisted of. She had grown up in a very sheltered Christian home in Denmark. She had never seen slums before. She had never even been drunk. So she asked the girls what life was like for them. All of a sudden they were the experts, not Hanne. It also made the girls much more willing to listen to Hanne when it came to sharing things she knew more about than they did.

What Every Young Person Needs

In the chapters to come, we'll examine seven general characteristics of today's at-risk teenagers and how each of these tends to influence their behavior. With Paul's letter to Philemon as a model, the chart on page 28 outlines each of these seven areas of need.

Whether you oversee a youth ministry of hundreds of teenagers, mentor a troubled teenager, teach junior high Sunday school, or lead a weekly Bible study at a detention center, the principles are the same. For teenagers to develop into healthy adults in Christ, seven basic needs must be met. The chapters to follow will describe each of them in detail and give ministry strategies for addressing those needs in youth ministry.

But let's begin by reading Paul's words to Philemon as he advocated for and described his relationship with Onesimus.

PHILEMON 10-18

I appeal to you for my son Onesimus, who became my son while I was in chains. Formerly he was useless to you, but now he has become useful both to you and to me. I am sending him—who is my very heart—back to you. I would have liked to keep him with me so that he could take your place in helping me while I am in chains for the gospel. But I did not want to do anything without your consent, so that any favor you do will be spontaneous and not forced. Perhaps the reason he was separated from you for a little while was that you might have him back for good—no longer as a slave, but better than a slave, as a dear brother. He is very dear to me but even dearer to you, both as a man and as a brother in the Lord.

So if you consider me a partner, welcome him as you would welcome me. If he has done you any wrong or owes you anything, charge it to me.

Endnotes

1. W. R. Gove and R. D. Cruthfield, "The Family and Juvenile Delinquency," The Sociological Quarterly, vol. 23 (1982), 301-319.

2. "Critical Criminal Justice Issues," Task Force Reports from the American Society of Criminology, compiled by National Institute of Justice, draft, (1996), 2.

3. William Barclay, *The Letters to Timothy, Titus, and Philemon*, rev. ed., (Philadelphia, PA: Westminster Press, 1975), 269.

4. Edgar J. Goodspeed, *An Introduction to the New Testament* (Chicago, IL: University of Chicago Press, 1937), 123.

5. Barclay, *The Letters to Timothy, Titus, and Philemon*, rev. ed., 270.

6. Barclay, *The Letters to Timothy, Titus, and Philemon*, rev. ed., 270.

7. Council on Crime in America, *Preventing Crime, Saving Children* (Center for Civic Innovation, Manhattan Institute, 1977),1-3.

8. There have been a number of cases of young people with juvenile records being banned from public high schools and colleges. For example, Massachusetts passed a law allowing public schools the option of banning youth with juvenile

records, and Harvard University expelled a student when they found out she had a juvenile record in Florida from years before.

9. David Smith, *The Life and Letters of St. Paul* (New York, NY: Harper and Brothers Publishers), 572-573.

10. In 1995 President Clinton declared juvenile crime to be the country's most serious crime problem. The State of America's Children Yearbook 1996 (The Children's Defense Fund, 1996), 58.

11. John Knox, *Philemon Among the Letters of Paul* (Chicago: University of Chicago Press, 1935), 54, and Goodspeed, *An Introduction to the New Testament,* 121-123.

Characteristics of a Mother or Father in Christ

For though you might have ten thousand guardians in Christ, you do not have many fathers. Indeed, in Jesus Christ I became your father through the gospel *(1 Corinthians 4:15, NRSV).*

PHILEMON 10-18

WHERE TEENAGERS ARE TODAY

CHARACTERISTICS OF TROUBLED YOUTH	BEHAVIOR PATTERN PRODUCED
VERSE 10 Because I have few positive adult role models...	I tend to reject authority, possess a deep-seated anger, have difficulty attaching, and struggle to express myself.
VERSE 11 Because I lack a biblical worldview...	I tend to be confused about what's right and wrong.
VERSE 11 Because I have become accustomed to failure...	I tend to fear success.
VERSE 12 Because I have experienced significant pain...	I tend to not trust anybody.
VERSE 13 Because I lack hope and a sense of purpose in my life...	I tend to not plan for tomorrow.
VERSES 15-16 Because I feel powerless, without many positive options...	I tend to rebel in unhealthy ways.
VERSE 18 Because I often have felt abandoned...	I tend to give up on myself too.

WHAT EVERY TEENAGER NEEDS

REMEDY REQUIRED	DESIRED RESULT
Therefore I need somebody to fill the role of a father or mother in Christ...	*so I can experience all I am as a full-fledged child of God.*
Therefore I need a genuine encounter with Christ and to see authentic faith lived out in someone...	*so I can reorient my life around that which works.*
Therefore I need to see myself as God sees me...	*so I can live in accordance with that identity.*
Therefore I need to feel I belong...	*so I can take risks to trust again.*
Therefore I need a dream or vision for my life...	*so I can make decisions with a long-term perspective.*
Therefore I need empowerment and healthy boundaries...	*so I can move toward healthy independence.*
Therefore I need at least one advocate who believes in me...	*so I can be a potential advocate for someone else.*

at Risk

What Every
Young Person
Needs to Become a
MATURE Adult
in
Christ

CHAPTER 3:
A Father or Mother in Christ

Because I have few positive adult role models, I tend to reject authority, possess a deep-seated anger, have difficulty attaching, and struggle to express myself. Therefore I need somebody to fill the role of a father or mother in Christ so I can experience all I am as a full-fledged child of God.

I appeal to you for my son Onesimus, who became my son while I was in chains (Philemon 10).

"Let me out of the car. I'm walking home! I hate you. I hate all of you, and I never want to see you again!" As Tina slammed the car door, she added, "I hope you die!"

Hanne had been elated about what God had done in Tina's life all week during the canoeing trip. But now Tina seemed to be distancing herself more than ever. Afraid of the decisions she was making for God and the relationships she was forming with Hanne and other adults, Tina was attempting to sabotage those relationships before they could hurt her, something she had grown all too accustomed to.

The work of developmental psychologist Erik Erikson helps shed light on such behavior. He defined eight stages of human psychological development. The first and most foundational is the ability to trust and form meaningful, bonding relationships. [1] When a child doesn't develop this capacity for whatever reason, distrust doesn't simply go away with age. Young people like Tina go through life longing for significant relationships but being deathly afraid of them at the same time. This very issue is at the core of much of the destructive behavior exhibited by at-risk youth. [2]

God's best design is to meet the developmental needs of children in the context of loving fathers and mothers, but not every family provides this. For many reasons, roughly half of all children in America don't live with both their biological parents. [3] Yet as we'll later examine, the roles that fathers and mothers should fill remain essential for children to develop into healthy adults.

While nobody can replace a missing parent, it is possible for somebody to provide some elements of that significant role. How can that role be best substituted? Someone can enter into the void and become a father or mother in Christ.

Long before Erik Erikson, the Apostle Paul knew the power of this kind of relationship and developed it with several people. Not only was he a father to a group of people in Corinth, but he also fulfilled that role in the lives of Timothy (1 Timothy 1:2), Titus (Titus 1:4), and Onesimus (Philemon 1:10). To the church in Thessalonica, he said, "We dealt with each of you as a *father* deals with his own children, encouraging, comforting and urging you to live lives worthy of God, who calls you into his kingdom and glory" (1 Thessalonians 2:11-12, author's emphasis).

This role is not exclusively masculine. Notice how Paul describes his dealings with the Thessalonians in another instance: "We were gentle among you, like a *mother* caring for her little children" (1 Thessalonians 2:7, author's emphasis). Likewise, when Jesus looked out over Jerusalem, he said, "How often I have longed to gather your children together, as a hen gathers her chicks under her wings, but you were not willing!" (Luke 13:34)

Scripture is filled with parental imagery used to describe the love and care God has for us and the level of commitment God asks us to extend toward others. Being a father or mother in Christ, then, represents a level of discipleship as well as the fulfillment of a specific role.

Let's now examine the importance of the father and mother roles and what typically happens to teenagers when a father or mother's influence is either negative or altogether absent.

The Need for a Father in Christ

While *both* mothers and fathers are necessary for healthy development of children, our culture is severely lacking in positive males when it comes to troubled teenagers. I once asked a group of guys in jail if any of them knew one positive man in his neighborhood he looked up to. They all thought hard for a few minutes; then each shook his head no.

WHEN A POSITIVE FATHER ROLE IS MISSING

In working with at-risk youth, I have observed two primary traits often present in those who grow up without a positive father-figure: hatred for authority and deep-seated anger.

HATRED FOR AUTHORITY

Hatred for authority is almost always present in teenagers when the authority figure of a father is either absent or abusive. Consequently, when a teacher says, "Sit down," they stand up. They hate the principal, the coach, and the police. They eventually hate their bosses at work, their probation officers—anyone who takes on the role of an authority figure in their life.

When we began taking into our home boys who were coming out of prison, I remember being confused. Why did they like me when I visited them in jail but suddenly began to dislike me once we took them into our home? I would sometimes ask if anything was wrong, if I had offended them in some way.

They would say no because even they didn't understand why their feelings toward me had changed. In time I began to realize that it's normal for young people to subconsciously transfer the hatred they hold toward their fathers onto anyone who begins to fill that role in their lives.

DEEP-SEATED ANGER

Deep anger is the second trait usually present in teenagers who grow up without positive father-figures. The Bible refers to this kind of anger as rage. I often see it displayed in the eyes of youth when we begin talking about fathers. In fact, in all my years ministering in prisons, I have met very few who didn't either hate or greatly dislike their fathers.

Each year Hallmark donates cases of cards for the teenagers to give away—birthday cards, Mother's and Father's Day cards, Christmas cards, and get well cards. They all go quickly—except the Father's Day cards. Almost no one has ever taken those.

Anger Thermometers—I sometimes ask teenagers to imagine that they have "anger thermometers" inside them that read "zero" when no anger is present and "ten" when they're over the edge and out of control.

"What does your thermometer read when you're not upset at anything in particular?" I ask. Most say it never goes below "seven" or "eight."

If someone looks at one of these young people angrily or stares suspiciously at them when passing on the street, this might send them up two or three notches on an anger thermometer. That's no problem if a person is at "zero" to begin with. But if the person is already at "eight," all of a sudden he or she is out of control, and somebody's going to get hurt. When I ask teenagers how many of them committed their crimes when they were at "ten," the majority raise their hands.

Where is all this anger coming from? Based on my experience, I believe that most deep-seated anger comes from being rejected by someone close to us, often in childhood. Is the cure more prisons, tougher laws, and stiffer punishments? Will that ever be effective in lowering the overall anger level of a rage-filled teenager? Quite the contrary. Most people leave prison with far more anger and a much greater hatred for authority than ever.

If the root of the problem is *rejection,* then the solution must be *acceptance,* but not just the bland statement, "I accept you as you are," which is closer to apathy and indifference. Rather, it's the kind of acceptance that God extends toward us.

Constraint Versus Restraint—One night several boys tried to escape from a detention center where we were leading a Bible study. Fortunately, everyone was caught and nobody was hurt. But as a result, all the participants were locked in their rooms for the next three weeks. Food was brought in to them, and they were allowed out of their rooms only to go to the bathroom and to shower. All their furniture was removed. Their rooms were bare except for a mattress on the floor.

Jose, who had been attending our Bible study, was one of those locked in his room. During that third week of isolation, Jose cracked. He asked a staff member if I could come in and visit him.

When I entered his room, I wasn't prepared for what I saw. Jose was standing in the corner of the room with his back against the wall. He was banging the wall with the back of his head and his clenched fist, over and over again. His face was so contorted with anger that he couldn't even focus on the fact that I was in the room.

I watched him for a little while, not really knowing what to say or do. Then gently, I put my arm around him. As I began to pull him toward me, Jose started hitting *my chest* instead of the wall. He wasn't trying to hurt me—he just needed an outlet for his anger and frustration.

I kept my arms around him until eventually his blows became softer and softer. Then Jose started to cry, and for the first time we actually made eye contact.

"I just need you to pray for me," he sobbed. "I've blown it so bad. I've let everyone down—my family, the staff, you, God—everybody."

I suggested he say those same things to God directly. He did, and it was one of the most beautiful prayers I'd ever heard. I'm sure this was the first time in three weeks that Jose had felt at peace.

A verse came to my mind later that night: "The love of Christ constraineth us" (2 Corinthians 5:14a, King James Version). "Constraint" is a word we don't hear very often today. It means "to hold together," "to keep in," "to be taken with." [4] What a marvelous depiction of what God does with us.

Psalm 139:17-18 tells how God's thoughts turn toward us continuously. Even when we're at our worst, God gives us his best. Though we may give up on God, God never gives up on us. Yes, even when we're faithless, God remains faithful, according to 2 Timothy 2:13. He doesn't treat us as we deserve. As a friend of mine was fond of saying, "God always deals with us within the confines of his hug." In a small way, that's what I did with Jose that night.

Somehow some of Jose's hurt and anger needed to flow into the life of another person for it to be released from him. Simply hitting a wall couldn't diffuse it. Sitting in a room by himself only made it worse. Yet as he struck me, someone who loved and accepted him anyway, the anger began to dissipate.

The analogy is consistent with Scripture. Jesus, on the cross, took the brunt of our sin, rage, and pain. "He was pierced for our transgressions, he was crushed for our iniquities" (Isaiah 53:5a). Even today, God is big enough to take our worst upon himself. God becomes the outlet for our anger. And somehow, in the process, knowing that God keeps holding us even while we're beating on him, the anger thermometer begins to go down—from "seven" to "six"—from "six" to "four." It's God's love that constrains us, that holds us together. "The punishment that brought us peace was upon him, and by his wounds we are healed" (Isaiah 53:5b).

This image is different from *restraint,* the approach most commonly applied to teenagers when they get out of control. Restraint means "to deprive of liberty," "to hold back," "to limit." Restraint rarely lowers the anger level in a teenager. It can't touch his or her need for acceptance and unconditional love.

Unfortunately, many liken God's dealings with us more to *restraint* than to *constraint.* Our teenagers need to experience the *true* love of God, often through us as vessels, holding them, being an outlet for their rage, constraining them.

Hanne is the best example of this I know. I remember watching her interactions with girls in the housing projects in Minneapolis where she ministered before we were married. They often abused her verbally. Sometimes they would say things like, "I hate you and never want to see you again!" I asked her why she kept working with them.

"Their anger isn't directed at me," she'd say. "Sometimes I'm just a safe place for them to vent it." Somehow Hanne was able (most of the time) to not take it personally when hurting teenage girls dished out their worst.

And over time, I saw the effect that had on those girls. Slowly the anger in some of them began to drain as they experienced a person who knew them at their worst, yet still loved them. And although Hanne hasn't lived in Minnesota for many years, she still receives calls and letters from many of those girls whose lives have been affected forever by her love and acceptance.

One such phone call recently came from Tina, the girl mentioned at the beginning of this chapter. "I just wanted you to know how often I think about you, Hanne. I have three kids of my own now. I want to raise them the way God wants me to, but most of the time I feel at a loss when it comes to knowing what God would want me to do. That's when I think of you. I ask myself, 'What would Hanne do?' and then I know that's probably what God would want.'"

The Need for a Mother in Christ

Kids need not only a father in Christ, but also a mother. In fact, a mother is the most important person in a child's life, particularly during the early years of childhood.

But a mother's influence doesn't end with the toddler stage. In juvenile jails, we conduct a Bible study on heroes, and we ask young people to name their greatest heroes. While one might expect to hear the names of professional athletes or musicians, almost without exception, young people say either "my mother" or "my grandmother."

Mothers are equally as important to a young person's understanding of the character of God as are fathers. In fact, one of the Old Testament names for God, "El Shaddai," is derived from the Hebrew noun *shad,* which is literally translated "breast." [5] All that a mother is to her baby, El Shaddai is to God's children, supplying sustenance, strength, satisfaction, and sufficiency as is beautifully illustrated in Isaiah 66:10-13. The most tender title used for God, the name El Shaddai describes his more nurturing motherly attributes: "As a mother comforts her child, so will I comfort you" (Isaiah 66:13a).

Recently I was trying to explain to a group of teenagers in jail what God is like. "God is a father who thinks about you continuously, who loves you no matter what you've done, who wants nothing more than to just be with you..."

As I was struggling for the next descriptive phrase, one of the boys finished my sentence: "...who's just like your mother." All the boys nodded in understanding.

WHEN A POSITIVE MOTHER ROLE IS MISSING

Just as a child is damaged by a missing father-figure, a missing mother-figure has negative effects as well. We've had three boys live with us who were abandoned by their mothers as infants. No doubt they were more damaged and maladjusted than any of the other teenagers who have lived with us.

It has been my experience that a mother's absence, at the very least, manifests itself in a detachment from close relationships and significantly stunted communication skills.

DETACHMENT FROM CLOSE RELATIONSHIPS

Maternal care and affection, especially in the early years of a child's life, are critical for a child to form significant, bonding relationships later in life.

Reggie had been abandoned by his mother as an infant. Growing up without either parent, he was moved from foster home to foster home, many of them abusive.

At age seventeen, Reggie moved into our house after he was released from a juvenile jail. We never felt as though Reggie really attached to us or invested in our home. His detachment probably was due to a combination of several factors. First, he didn't know us very well before he moved in, so he hadn't yet developed a trust for us. Second, there were five other boys living with us at the time, so he didn't get much one-on-one attention.

But perhaps the biggest reason was that Reggie never had experienced real family attachment before. He almost seemed to lack the capacity for it. After living with us for about four months, Reggie completely sabotaged our relationship, leaving on bad terms. His future looked grim. We expected never to hear from him again.

Then about a year later he contacted us. Surprisingly, he had gotten off drugs, and he had a good job. What had happened to him?

Laura, one of Reggie's middle school teachers, had kept in contact with him, on and off, since he had been in her class. All the while he was in and out of detention centers and foster homes, Laura had been a stable force.

Though she rarely saw him and spoke with him only by phone every few months, she was the most consistent component in his tumultuous life. After Reggie left our home, he bounced from living with friends to homeless shelters to county jails, but all the while he kept in contact with Laura.

When Reggie finally hit bottom and was ready to make a change, he knew whom to call. She was able to help him get a job and find a place to live, and she continued to be there as a support. Without her, I don't think Reggie would have made it.

Reggie said as much. "Whenever I think of a mother, I think of Laura. I guess she really is my mother. She's already proven to me that she'll be there for me, no matter what. I think I'm gonna make it OK."

I think so too. It seems that a kid can make it through almost anything if he or she has at least one person who's there no matter what happens. Usually it's a mother. That's what it took for a seemingly hopeless kid like Reggie.

A word of caution here. Generally, I wouldn't recommend a woman investing to that level in the life of a teenage boy or a man in the life of a teenage girl. The roles can become confused, and young people can easily develop unhealthy feelings and attractions for any adults who take on this role in their lives. When it comes to troubled teenagers, it usually is best for women to minister to girls and men to boys. The exceptions are senior adults who take on grandparent roles or married couples who minister together. This worked particularly well in the life of Jimmy.

We first met Jimmy when he came to one of our Bible studies. He beamed from ear to ear when he found out we knew Rick and Lori. They were the leaders of the Bible study Jimmy had attended at another detention center a few years earlier.

"Rick and Lori are like a mom and dad to me, you know." Jimmy excitedly reported.

"Really? What makes you say that?" we asked.

"Well, no matter where I end up, they keep writing to me. They give me Bible verses to read and always say they're praying for me. I guess they've just always been there for me.

"Then last week it was my birthday. I didn't get a cake or a phone call from anybody. I was real down. But Rick and Lori remembered, and they sent me a card. Here, you want to see it? They're just like parents to me."

Being a father or mother in Christ doesn't mean you have to see a young person every day. It doesn't mean you have to take a teenager into your home. Often it's just being mindful of little things, like sending a birthday card or making an occasional phone call or visit, that lets a young person know there's somebody out there who cares. For some teenagers this can mean the difference between feeling like a nobody and feeling as though they're important to somebody. And that can make all the difference in the world.

STUNTED COMMUNICATION SKILLS

A second detrimental effect of growing up without a healthy mother is often revealed in a young person's lack of good communication skills. Researchers say that mothers generally have more influence than fathers on the way children come to think and behave in relating to people. [6]

Mothers and fathers in Christ need to understand some of the issues that affect the communication skills of all youth. Teenagers in general have become less proficient in the art of communication. Twenty years ago, if you chaperoned a bus load of teenagers, the noise level was deafening with talking, singing, and screaming. Today the same bus may well be virtually quiet. Why? Everyone is listening to personal stereos or playing video games.

Technology and the media definitely have had an impact on our present generation of teenagers. Though a noisy bus load of teenagers doesn't necessarily indicate quality communication, it does indicate that young people are actively engaged with one another. Contrarily, as a result of millions of images being continually flashed before them through television, movies, music videos, video games, and computers, young people have become much more passive in how they learn and process information. [7]

Not only have media caused youth to become more passive in how they learn, but their attention spans have become much shorter as well. Rent a movie sometime that was produced more than twenty-five years ago, and notice how different it is from those produced today. It's obvious that today's movies are created to appeal to people with shorter attention spans. In the older movies, the camera remains on a person or scene for several seconds. In today's movies, the camera never focuses on one angle or image for more than a second or two.

Then there was the introduction of the remote control—in my opinion the greatest invention in recent history. It allows me to watch two programs at the same time, something I love to do but have given up on since it's also one of the greatest sources of conflict in our marriage.

This device has programmed young people to decide what they'll watch in seconds, as they quickly scan dozens of channels. As a result of all this technology, many of our young people literally *can't* focus on anything for more than a few minutes. It means we have to be much more creative in our programming and not simply lecture. Most young people today just don't have the capacity to process information delivered in that format.

How does that affect their ability to communicate? For one thing, young people have become accustomed to engaging in several activities at the same time. How often have you seen teens sitting in the same room with their friends, talking but never looking at each other? The reason is simple: The TV is on and their eyes are riveted to it, rather than to one another. While the avoidance of eye contact may tend to make them feel more comfortable with one another, it has a negative effect on the development of their social skills. [8]

And finally, many teenagers growing up in a media culture have developed an unhealthy bond with television. *Sesame Street* and Barney are perhaps the most popular baby sitters in contemporary culture. They're called upon for their services many times each day; in fact, the average preschooler in America watches twenty-seven hours of television per week. [9] As a result, countless children have formed attachments to characters such as Big Bird, who then become some of their primary teachers, through whom they learn and experience much of life. Research has shown that the average child gets more one-on-one attention from TV than from all her parents and teachers combined. [10]

This attachment carries on into the teenage years, making it quite natural for teenagers to look to talk shows, MTV, and sitcoms to educate them about life. And because it is one-way learning and not interactive, youth are deprived of learning healthy communication skills, skills that come through interacting with people, not videos.

As Reginald Bibby and Donald Posterski explain in *Teen Trends,* "Television certainly links people together, but the connectedness is really impersonal and artificial. In the end, instead of enhancing person-to-person life, television can [actually] impinge on real relationships." [11]

The problem of poor communication skills is compounded for a teenager who grows up without a healthy relationship with his or her mother. Couple TV's influence with a young person's growing up without healthy verbal interaction, and you find yourself dealing with a "social vegetable," someone who feels all the frustration of stress but lacks the relational connectedness with which to work through it. It's not that there aren't people around; it's that they've never learned to really communicate with them. Lonely and isolated, these teenagers almost have no choice but to act on the destructive realities of what they see and hear through television and music. To them, that is the real world.

A Mother's Role in Developing Healthy Communication—A child's adeptness in communicating directly reflects the quality of time spent with his or her mother. Even on into the teenage years, it's usually the mother who communicates best with kids. Why? Partly because she tends to be around more, and partly because women tend to be better at communicating in nonjudgmental ways. [12]

Hanne is the one who has most of the really good talks with the guys in our home. They feel they can tell her anything, and they do. I communicate with them too, but it's more difficult for me to get past the "to-do lists" I have for them or reviewing the "checklists" I previously had assigned them. I have to work hard to get past the level of sharing mere facts and information and move to a level where real communication happens.

John Powell, in his classic book *Why Am I Afraid to Tell You Who I Am?* defines five levels of communication. [13] At the most detached level he describes level-five relationships. Communication here consists largely of things like "How are you doing?" and "What's happening?" To these questions, the desired and appropriate answers always are "Fine" and "Not much." These questions are asked in passing and without any desire or expectation of an honest answer.

Level-four relationships aren't much deeper, as they expose nearly nothing of ourselves. Here we merely exchange information. We talk about the weather or a sporting event on television last night. Level-four friendships are like the evening news, concerned primarily with facts. And while it's safe communication, in and of itself, it isn't all that gratifying. It gives nothing of ourselves, nor does it invite anything from others in return.

In level-three relationships, we begin to communicate more of who we are. It involves the risk of telling some of our ideas, judgments, and opinions. As I begin to tell you what I think, there is the possibility that you may not agree—thus, the risk of potential rejection.

Level-two communication really happens at the gut level. It is here that I move from telling you what's in my head to what's in my heart. It moves from telling my thoughts to revealing my feelings. To tell you my *thoughts* is to locate myself in a *category*, but to tell my *feelings* is to tell you about me.

Level-one communication is completely open and transparent in every dimension. It usually is reserved for good marriages or one or two very close friends.

It's been my observation that men tend to communicate most often at levels four and five, and sometimes at level three. Women, on the other hand, are usually better at communicating at the deeper levels. It is critically important for teenagers to experience communication at the second and third levels to develop effective communication skills.

When a mother spends significant amounts of time dialoguing with her children about what they think about various issues and helping them to process and talk about their feelings, she is granting them an invaluable gift.

So what can be done for those young people who haven't been so fortunate, who haven't experienced what healthy communication is all about?

Developing Healthy Communication—Small-group interaction is an essential part of any effective youth ministry today. At first it can be threatening, as teenagers often don't know what to say or how to healthily debate and discuss topics. But it has been my experience that it just takes practice. When you provide a safe environment where teenagers can freely express themselves without fear of being put down, they begin to flourish.

For troubled teenagers, the need to relate primarily within the context of a small group or in a one-on-one relationship is even greater. Many feel uncomfortable in large-group events, whether it be a youth group meeting or a church service. And for many, the only times they've been vocal about their feelings is when they've been drunk or high. They need to learn to trust and communicate positively in a small-group setting before they're willing to risk moving into a larger group.

What Youth Need to Hear From a Mother or Father in Christ

Being loved and embraced by one's father and mother is such a deep, God-given need that even Jesus, the perfect son of God, was twice publicly granted some critically important words of affirmation from his father. God said, "This is *my Son*, whom *I love*; with him I am *well pleased*" (Matthew 3:17 and 17:5, author's emphasis).

These three things are essential for every son or daughter to hear: "This is my son (or daughter)," "I love you," and "I'm proud of you." If a young person doesn't hear these things from a biological mom and dad, then he or she needs to hear them from a mother or father in Christ.

WHAT'S SO SPECIAL ABOUT A NAME?

Speaking at a men's retreat, I asked how many participants could recall their fathers addressing them as "son." Less than half raised their hands. For a boy to be called son, especially by his father, is so significant. Although it doesn't sound as natural for a girl to be addressed as "daughter," having a special name that applies only to her is every bit as important, hence, the need for nicknames.

Hanne and I each give nicknames to every boy who moves into our house. Some of mine might sound a little strange to you, but Calvin is Cal-Dawg, Jay is JayBird, Brian is Byron, Felix—Felicimo. You get the point. Whenever I call their names, they know who's calling. I've given them names, and I'm the only one who calls them by those names. Because I play the role of a father in their lives, hearing those names from me gives them a great sense of identity and security, a sense of importance.

Give personal nicknames to the teenagers you work with closely. Take it seriously. Once you give them nicknames, even if you forget the names, they won't. They'll beg you (often without verbalizing it) to remember and call them by those names again.

For those you don't know as well, make it a priority to remember their names. Names represent something of a person's identity. When you remember young people's names, that speaks loudly to them. It helps them believe they're important in your eyes.

God's big on names too. Back in the Garden of Eden, the only names God assigned were to God's children, Adam and Eve. None of the animals were given personal names. God knows each of us by name, too. John 10:3 declares, "He calls his own sheep by name and leads them out." God even says that our names have been written in the "Lamb's book of life" (Revelation 21:27).

Perhaps one day when you hear God call your name, you'll suddenly recognize it as one that has resonated deep within your spirit from eternity past—not your parent-given name, but the one God gave you before the foundation of the world. You'll know it and be glad.

LOVE MUST BE SPOKEN

The second thing Jesus heard from his Father was the phrase "whom I love." Undoubtedly, three of the most powerful words in our language are "I love you."

We were celebrating Craig's birthday at the end of one of our detention center Bible studies. I was thinking about how much growth we had seen in his life since we met three years earlier. In many ways, I felt as if I had watched him grow up in that institution. As we were standing up to leave the room, I hugged him and said, "You know, Craig, I really love you."

His eyes started to tear up, and then his body began shaking. It was an awkward situation for him. Everyone was lining up for dinner except Craig. He didn't want to walk out of the room and be embarrassed.

Finally, as he regained some composure, he said, "You know what? You're the *first* person who's ever told me that." One phrase had completely wiped out this otherwise rough and tough kid.

On another occasion, I had taken a few of the guys from our home with me on a youth retreat where I was speaking. After one session, Nathan hung around while I was talking to some other youth. I was mindful of his presence and the fact that he didn't seem to want to leave. At one point I turned around, put my arm around him, and said, "I love you, Nate." He didn't say anything, and I didn't think any more about it.

I was out of town that next week. When I phoned home on Wednesday evening, the Bible study at our house was just finishing up. Hanne told me how Nathan (usually the quiet one when it comes to sharing at Bible study) talked for most of the time about how I had told him that I loved him. He went into great detail about the whole evening, explaining all that had led up to my telling him I loved him and what happened after that. I was reminded again of the powerful force of blessing and healing we hold—and of how often we withhold it.

Growing up, I always knew my dad loved me. There was never any doubt about it in my mind. I just don't remember his ever saying it. I'm sure he probably did when I was young, but I can't remember ever hearing it. That's not all that unusual. Like many men, he probably never heard it from his dad, who likely never heard it from his. Besides, it can feel awkward for a man to say, "I love you" to his teenage or grown son.

I remember one particular telephone conversation my dad and I had several years ago, while I was living in another state. As we were about to hang up, I felt impressed to tell him I loved him. It was one of those times when I acted on impulse and said, "I love you." He paused for a moment, and then he said, "I love you, too."

That was a pretty big moment for us. I don't think we've had a phone conversation since that hasn't ended with his saying, "I love you." Sometimes I almost make a game of it, seeing if I can hang up the phone before he's able to say it.

"Well, dad, gotta go, see ya."

"Wa- wa-...wait...," he'll say. "I love you."

"I love you too, dad."

All those years, I think he really wanted to say it. He just didn't know how. It took my initiating it. That's how it often is with these words. They're awkward to say the first time. But they're so very important. Someone has to take the risk and be the first to say them. And the rewards are always well worth the risk.

Again, it's important that men share this powerful experience primarily with boys and women primarily with girls to avoid the confusion that young people can experience with the opposite sex.

JUST SAY IT!

The last part of the Father's public statement to Jesus was "With him I am well pleased." What impact the words "I'm proud of you" can have. Though kids need to hear it from both fathers and mothers, for some reason most fathers tend to be a little slower at dispensing it.

Hanne has said on many occasions, "I talk to the guys about almost everything, and it means a lot to them when I say I'm proud of them. They like it. But what they really need—what they crave—is Scott's approval." Why? Because most of them have never heard those words from a father before. Most likely the youth you're working with haven't either.

The sad thing is that Hanne's approval comes so much freer and more frequently than does mine. We all need to work on freely and liberally dispensing the words "I'm proud of you." For when we withhold them, we not only prevent healing, but we also can inflict serious damage.

Three Things Every Mother or Father in Christ Should Know

For anyone who considers becoming a mother or father in Christ to a young person, here are three challenges to be aware of.

SABOTAGE

Don't be surprised when teenagers begin trying to sabotage your relationship just when it seems things are beginning to go well. This often means they're getting ready to really invest, but they're afraid of getting hurt again. Important authority figures have hurt them too many times in the past. They want to make sure they can trust you before they begin investing too much.

JUSTIN

Justin had lived with us for more than two years. He was more articulate: "I've been hurt so many times that I'll hurt you before you have a chance to hurt me." Teenagers like this have a not-so-subtle way of sabotaging every significant relationship they enter. And often it becomes a self-fulfilling prophecy that leads them to conclude, "See, I knew you'd just leave me anyway."

What Justin needed was one person who would stay with him long enough to replace his image of a negative authority figure. Then slowly, a new, more positive image could be created in its place. This in turn could open him up to being able to accept other authorities in his life, including God.

COMMITMENT

Make every attempt to stick to your commitment, even when a teenager doesn't stick to his or her commitment. This obviously is easier said than done.

ALEX

Jim had agreed to mentor fifteen-year-old Alex. The experience wasn't all he had envisioned, though. It wasn't that they didn't click. It was that they didn't *meet!* Every time Jim went to Alex's house to pick him up as agreed, Alex wasn't home. This happened seven times in a row! The next time Jim was driving to Alex's, he already had decided this was the last chance he was giving the relationship. It seemed more than obvious that Alex just wasn't interested. After ringing the doorbell several times, Jim walked back to his car, knowing he wouldn't come back again.

Just as he was about to drive away, Alex yelled out a bedroom window, "Wait!" and came running out to the car. That day, the two of them began a friendship that would last several years. Jim later learned that Alex had been watching him from his window each time he came. He was testing Jim's commitment before he was going to invest. In Jim's case, *showing up* was *more* than half the battle.

Every time you make a commitment to a young person and then keep it, even when the young person breaks his or her commitment, you make major strides toward rebuilding the image of a positive authority figure. Why? Because the role you play as a significant, caring adult counteracts the influence of all the other adults who may have dropped the ball with them over the years.

And although a series of failed relationships may contribute to a young person's distrust toward adults who "get too close," experiencing a successful relationship with an adult who keeps commitments can begin to reverse all that.

Hanne used to tell the volunteer mentors that she supervised, "You have to expect to phone a girl ten times in order to reach her once. Don't view it as wasted time. On the contrary, it often works to strengthen the relationship as nothing else can." There are simply no shortcuts for this one.

ROUGH TIMES

Realize that rough times are often the essential building blocks of long-term trust. None of us likes to invest in a relationship that constantly seems to be in turmoil or conflict. I, for one, hate conflict. But I've come to see how conflict, when resolved properly, does more than almost anything else to build a positive relationship. It's during this period in a relationship that teenagers discern whether we're really committed to them or not.

Most troubled teens have had few positive experiences with resolving conflict. Either conflict has resulted in violence, or at the least, the relationship has ended. Working with a young person to resolve conflicts exposes them to a whole new model upon which they can build. It proves to the young person that you're not going to walk away when things get tough.

At the same time, it's important to be honest with young people when you feel frustrated about irresponsibility or an apparent lack of commitment. Appropriately expressing your frustrations lets a young person know that the relationship is important to you. And that goes a long way toward building mutual trust.

Summary

In this chapter we've dealt with what it means to be a mother or father in Christ to an at-risk teenager.

Being a mother or father in Christ...

IS NOT • **attempting to replace the young person's parents**—We never will replace a teenager's parents nor should we attempt to. In fact, it's very detrimental even to speak negatively about a young person's parents when the teenager can hear you. Even if the teenager speaks negatively about the parents, he or she won't accept it from anyone else. Nothing will drive a wedge between you and that young person faster.

Many of these parents are doing the best job they know how. Some have done a very good job; they just need more support. Rather than tearing down parents, we must build upon the good they have done. Often it's the community and the peers who have influenced the young person negatively.

Gaining credibility with the family is also crucial. Without it, parents often will sabotage what you're attempting to do. Sometimes this is out of jealousy, sometimes because of misunderstanding. Whenever you work with at-risk teenagers, that work needs to ultimately carry over into their families to be most effective.

Shari's family was cold toward Hanne for years. Nothing she did seemed to help them accept her and not be threatened by her—until she offered to start giving free haircuts to family members. That was the bridge that made it possible for Hanne to minister to three other sisters and ultimately have access to the entire family.

IS NOT • **assuming responsibility for a young person and the family**—Most at-risk youth have very complicated lives. It's unlikely that you alone will be able to undo all the damage that has been done. As a rule, you shouldn't get involved in financially subsidizing their needs or having the young person move into your home. Ideally, there are many people involved in this young person's life—social workers, counselors, family service agencies, or welfare workers. It's important to realize what role God is asking you to play and what God isn't asking you to do.

IS NOT · **meeting our own needs**—I once heard someone ask a pointed question to a group of ministry leaders: "Do you need a ministry more than God needs another minister?" It's a question that deserves our consideration. When *we* need to be needed as much as the youth we're working with need us, we're embarking on dangerous ground. At best it's a case of codependency; at worst, spiritual manipulation.

Being a mother or father in Christ...

IS · **a level of commitment and discipleship that goes beyond that of just another guide**—You can't provide that in a great number of teenagers' lives, but most at-risk teenagers desperately need at least one individual (outside their immediate families) who will provide this in their lives. As a youth worker, it's your job to help find mature Christian adults who are called and willing to fulfill this role in the lives of teenagers. You also should pray about whom God may want you to adopt as a Timothy, Titus, or Onesimus in your own life.

We cannot give this level of discipleship to young people if we never have received it ourselves, however. Do you have a father or mother in Christ? Is there a "Paul" in your life? If you oversee a ministry, do each of your volunteers have a "Paul" in their lives? It takes healthy parents to produce healthy children. One of the first things you may need to do is make sure you and your staff are receiving this level of discipleship before you attempt to pass it on to young people.

IS · **building a foundation of trust and relationship**—These are two ingredients that are necessary if we're going to see positive changes take place in the lives of hurting young people.

State officials have occasionally questioned whether we have adequate staff supervision in our homes. At times they have encouraged us to move toward a more "structured program" model versus the "family" paradigm we use. But a program by itself doesn't make a young person more safe. Trust and relationship are the only things we have to hold youth. Even the most secure prison in the world isn't safe without trust and relationship between staff and inmates.

Erik Erikson has pointed out that unless the issue of trust is resolved for a young person, that person will remain stunted in emotional (and spiritual) development. Honesty, consistency, and a stable presence through both good and bad times are what lay the critical foundation of trust. Our role is not to fix teenagers but to be there for them. And this, over time, will lay a foundation for God to bring into their lives others with whom they can build relationships of trust as well.

• **an opportunity to experience a spiritual family**—Whenever anyone becomes a Christian, that person becomes a full-fledged son or daughter of God, a fellow heir with Jesus, and a member of the family of God. Most at-risk teens, however, have a severely distorted concept of family. They need to experience firsthand what healthy families look and feel like.

Brothers and sisters in Christ are critical, but often brother- and sister-relationships are possible only when people have experienced what fathers or mothers in Christ are. I'm convinced that the family is the paradigm through which spiritual truth is best taught and understood.

ENDNOTES

1. Erik H. Erikson, *The Life Cycle Completed* (New York: W. W. Norton & Co., 1982), 56-60.

2. For a fuller description of the phases of adolescent development, see *Quick Connect*, written by Scott Larson, Dave Van Patten, and Alexander Dunlop, to be published by Group Publishing in 2000.

3. Linda Nielson, *Adolescence: A Contemporary View*, 3rd ed. (Fort Worth, TX: Harcourt Brace College Publishers, 1996), 350.

4. James Strong, "Greek Dictionary of the New Testament," *Strong's Exhaustive Concordance* (Gordonsville, TN: Dugan Publishers, Inc.), 69.

5. James Strong, "Hebrew and Chaldee Dictionary," *The Exhaustive Concordance of the Bible* (New York, NY: Abingdon-Cokesbury Press, 1890), 112-113.

6. Nielson, *Adolescence: A Contemporary View*, 315.

7. Nielson, *Adolescence: A Contemporary View*, 90.

8. Reginald W. Bibby and Donald C. Posterski, *Teen Trends: A Nation in Motion* (Toronto: Stoddart Publishing Co., 1992), 281.

9. David Grossman, "Trained to Kill," Christianity Today (August 10, 1998), 38.

10. Grossman, "Trained to Kill," 38.

11. Bibby and Posterski, *Teen Trends: A Nation in Motion*, 281.

12. Nielson, *Adolescence: A Contemporary View*, 315.

13. John Powell, *Why Am I Afraid to Tell You Who I Am?* (Chicago, IL: Argus Communications, 1969), 54-61.

YOUTH MINISTRY EVALUATION

Providing Fathers and Mothers in Christ

Rate your youth ministry in each of the following areas by circling the appropriate number.

1   **2**   **3**   **4**   **5**

The proportion of male and
female leaders is lopsided
in ratio to the teenagers.

The proportion of male and
female leaders is about equal
in ratio to the teenagers.

1   **2**   **3**   **4**   **5**

Our program tends to be content-
oriented more than relational.

Our program is as relationship-
based as it is content-based.

1   **2**   **3**   **4**   **5**

Most of our youth don't participate
in weekly small groups or in
one-to-one adult discipleship
relationships.

Nearly all our youth are in
weekly small groups or
one-to-one adult discipleship
relationships.

1   **2**   **3**   **4**   **5**

Our leaders typically don't
include the youth in the lives
of their families.

Most of our youth leaders
include the youth in the
lives of their families.

1   **2**   **3**   **4**   **5**

Most of our youth leaders
don't have "mother or
father in Christ" relationships.

Nearly all our youth leaders are
receiving in-depth discipleship
themselves.

Total score: _____ (enter this score in the scoring key on page 132.)

CHAPTER 4:
A Genuine Encounter With Christ

Because I lack a biblical worldview, I tend to be confused about what's right and wrong. Therefore I need a genuine encounter with Christ and to see authentic faith lived out in someone so I can reorient my life around that which works.

Formerly he was useless to you, but now he has become useful both to you and to me (Philemon 11).

"Is it just me, or are all the colors in here all of a sudden bright?" exclaimed Raphael.

"It's just you," I assured him. "Everything looks the same to me."

Raphael had just prayed to make a commitment to Jesus. We were in that same dingy-looking room we had been having Bible study in for years. The colors were as drab as gray gets. But it all looked different to him today.

Raphael had been attending the Bible study for several months, but he just couldn't believe that God could really care about him, much less love him.

"You've got to change yourself. God ain't going to do it," he would say. "I see kids coming to this Bible study all the time, getting into all that God stuff. But then when they get out, they just go right back to the same old stuff.

"I'm not going to be like that," he promised. "If I change, it'll be 'cause I want to change. Then I'll be the one to make it happen. And I'll stick to it too."

But then Raphael started to soften. He was approaching his release date, and it was obvious that he was getting scared. "I know I'm not going to make it out there," he confessed. "I really need God to help me. I want to ask God to be a part of my life."

And now Raphael was looking up from his prayer, beaming from ear to ear. To him, everything looked completely different. The colors were brighter, the room was bigger. He felt different. He could hardly believe it. At that moment, he *knew* God was real.

Today's young people need more than just to know *about* God. They need to encounter and experience God in a way that connects personally with them.

When I was in high school, we spent lots of time studying apologetics. We knew that if our friends were going to seriously consider the claims of Christ, we had to present logical arguments for our faith.

For teenagers living in these postmodern times, however, understanding isn't believing. Seeing or feeling is believing. Does that mean God must perform miracles on demand? Certainly not. But I have been somewhat surprised at how willing God is to meet young people right where they are and to reveal himself to them in just the way they need.

Duane

A few years ago, Duane was in one of our detention center Bible studies. "How do you know God's real?" he interrupted. "Nobody's ever seen God, right? Have you seen God?"

"No," Hanne responded, "I have never seen God. But I know God's real. And God promises that whoever really seeks God will find him. You just ask, Duane. God will show you, if you're really serious. But ultimately it will still take a step of faith for you to believe. The Bible says that without faith it's impossible to please God."

The next week when we came back to the Bible study, the group was already assembled and waiting for us. Duane was in the midst of telling the whole group about what had happened to him the week before.

"Last Wednesday after Bible study I went into my room to pray. I asked God to show me if he really was real. I had ten dimes on my dresser, and I told God that I would throw them all on the floor, and if they all landed heads-up, I would know God was real."

"Now wait a minute, Duane," we interrupted. "That's not what we were saying..."

Without hesitating to acknowledge our input, he continued, "After I threw them all on the floor, I started counting them. All ten dimes had landed heads-up! I started banging on my door for a staff person. 'God's real!' I told him. 'Can I call my grandmother? I've got to tell her that I know God's real! She's been praying for me for a long time. I have to tell her that now I know God's real!' "

Does God always respond this way? No, certainly not. In fact, we haven't heard of God doing "the dime thing" since. But there are many young people who genuinely are seeking God and who have no touch point with the message of Christ at all. And they need to know that God is real.

Throughout Scripture and church history, it has seemed that when God's Spirit was moving into new territories where the message of Christ had largely been absent, God often revealed himself in more dramatic ways. And the majority of at-risk teenagers are about as far removed from this message as any group can be.

Biblical Illiteracy

The majority of troubled teenagers today are two generations removed from anything remotely Christian. Fathers generally are out of the picture entirely, and most of the mothers possess only distant memories of authentic faith. Typically, a grandmother is the closest family link to vibrant Christianity.

It isn't uncommon to hear teenagers passionately describe their grandmothers' faith by saying, "My grandmother would pray for like six hours every day, read her Bible for four hours, and then go to church every night!"

We used to give out brightly colored, contemporary-looking Bibles. But teenagers would always say, "Don't you have any *real* Bibles? You know, the big black ones that say "Holy Bible" in gold letters—the kind like my Grandma had." Now we try to find modern translations packaged in more traditional-looking covers to give out.

While Grandma's authentic faith often is the reason teenagers are eager to turn to Christ during times of crisis, that doesn't mean the teenagers have much knowledge of Christ or the Scriptures. It's easy to assume that teenagers who grow up in America know something about God and the Bible, but often that's not the case.

Recently we were talking about the meaning of Christmas in a detention center Bible study. I asked if anyone knew when the first Christmas was. One of our "deacon-material" young people quickly raised his hand.

"It was in 1812!" he proudly blurted out. Hmm. Then I asked if anyone knew what Easter was all about.

Another boy, not wanting to be shown up, said, "Oh, that's Jesus' anniversary."

Another week we were showing the Christian movie *Fury to Freedom,* the dramatic story of Raul Ries, now a pastor in California. Raul was a troubled teenager who wanted nothing to do with God. He had won the heart of a Christian girl while in high school, but then he began bringing her down with him. In one of the scenes in the movie, his girlfriend finds out she's pregnant. She starts crying, repenting to God for what she's done. At that point in the movie there was a lot of confusion and chattering among the guys in the Bible study.

"Why is she crying?" somebody asked.

"Is it a sin to get pregnant?" questioned another.

Finally, Anthony, the spiritual giant of the group, who had been attending Bible study for several months, decided to end the confusion and clarify the biblical perspective. "She's crying because if you're a Christian, you can only have sex with other Christians."

The other boys all nodded, responding with "Oh..." Now they understood.

We decided to let the movie keep going and address that topic at another time.

Think about it. Where are these youth going to hear the most basic teachings on Christian faith or the meanings of Christian holidays? From their friends? in school? If they haven't heard the message at home, they probably know nothing about it.

Hanne once had a girl who looked very confused as they were reading the Bible in a detention center. Finally she rather sheepishly interrupted, "Is Jesus Christ a *real person?*"

"Yes, he is," answered Hanne. "Much of the Bible is about him."

"I never knew that. I always thought it was just a swear word."

Such ignorance is why it's imperative that we clearly teach young people even the most basic standards that God lays out for us, not assuming they know anything at all. And when we recite biblical stories, we must start at the beginning of the story and tell it all the way through. This also makes it more exciting. These teenagers don't already know the end of the story before you begin. They sit on the edge of their seats, asking, "Then what happened?"

At other times, their responses aren't what we might expect. Once after I had told the story of David slaying Goliath, a boy raised his hand. With a confused look, he asked, "So who was the good guy?" You have to tell the whole story when you teach the Bible to these teenagers. But I must confess, trying to give a coherent answer to that boy's question even had me a bit stumped.

Realizing how little these young people know about God can be very discouraging. How, in one hour a week, can we possibly communicate what is necessary for them to read and understand the Bible on their own? One night Eddie, a Hispanic boy, asked me for a Bible. He couldn't read

Spanish, so he asked me for an English one. I gave him one, but I was thinking, "How much is he going to get out of this book? He knows so little about God, and he doesn't even understand English all that well."

The next week when we came back, Eddie met us at the door. He thanked me over and over for the Bible, saying, "You know, this is a great book. And it's the first one I've ever been able to understand!" We must never give up on God's ability to transform a young person's life beyond all reasonable expectation.

The Role of an Ambassador

Sometimes God does move dramatically into a young person's life and reveal himself in a miraculous way. But more often, young people encounter the Living God through a loving, caring, committed Christian.

Brennan was a guy we gladly would have missed had he quit showing up at the Bible study we were leading. He always seemed to get us off track with statements like "I follow Satan, and he's stronger than God!"

We tried to keep loving Brennan, but for the weeks he attended, none of the Bible studies went particularly well, largely because of his comments.

Then one week when we arrived, we were met by a completely different Brennan. As usual, he was the first to speak, but it was what he said that was so unusual. "Would it be OK if I opened us in prayer tonight?"

"What?" we thought. Then suspiciously we inquired, "Well, that depends on who you want to pray to, Brennan."

"Oh, I want to pray to Jesus," he beamed.

After the Bible study we couldn't wait to pull him aside. "What happened to you, Brennan?"

"I accepted Jesus into my life."

Not sounding too convinced, we continued to probe: "But why? What in the world made you change your mind?"

"Well, seeing you both come in here week after week, loving me no matter how much of a jerk I was—that really blew me away. No one's ever treated me like that before. I knew there must be a God.

We were reminded of the verse "We are therefore Christ's ambassadors, as though God were making his appeal through us" (2 Corinthians 5:20). The dictionary defines an ambassador as a "resident representative of one's own sovereign for a special assignment." What a privilege and high responsibility we've been given!

The vast majority of those who become Christians do so because of the influence of people who took the time to love them with the love of Christ—to be ambassadors. This is what most often convinces people that there really is a God. Not only do we *have* the answer, but in many ways we *are* the answer. It's Christ in us, the hope of glory, that is God's primary method of reaching troubled teenagers (Colossians 1:27).

Danger–Beware!

It's imperative that every teenager experience a genuine encounter with Christ firsthand if he or she is to develop into a mature Christian. However, becoming a disciple of Jesus goes far beyond an *experience.* In fact, it's relatively easy for youth to make commitments to Christ. Many of them are hurting badly and are willing to try anything that might offer some relief. The greatest challenge is to see them grow to maturity in their faith.

When we invest significantly in the lives of troubled young people, we may encounter a subtle temptation to manipulate them spiritually. As teenagers begin to trust us, they often will do whatever we ask, wanting to please us. Yet unless they come to realize that Christ holds the answers for their lives, not us, they'll never grow to maturity.

Veteran gang youth worker Gordon McLean states, "Many high-risk youth who pray to receive Christ do so in an emotional emergency, seeing it as a type of 'good luck charm.' They need to mature in their character and understanding of the Gospel in order to make a life decision that they will uphold." [1]

Evangelism as a Process

In working with at-risk teenagers, I've found it helpful to view evangelism as a process or continuum. Many Christians tend to think only in terms of "before commitment" and "after commitment." This can cause people to feel that they haven't made real progress or shared their faith until they see someone praying to become a Christian.

This way of thinking can be particularly destructive when we're dealing with those who lack a foundational understanding of Christ and the Bible, as do the majority of troubled teenagers.

Francis Schaeffer, noted author and theologian, once was speaking to a group of theological students at Oxford University on the subject of communicating the message of Christ to those dominated by contemporary philosophy. A postgraduate student stood up and said, "Sir, if we understand you correctly, you are saying that pre-evangelism must come before evangelism. If this is so, then we have been making a mistake at Oxford. The reason we have not been reaching many of these people is because we have not taken enough time with pre-evangelism." With this, Schaeffer totally agreed. [2]

Evangelism is a process. And it's essential that we understand the place God is asking us to play in this process in the life of a young person, entrusting the rest to God. The Apostle Paul stated clearly, "I planted the seed, Apollos watered it, but God made it grow" (1 Corinthians 3:6). We don't all need to be the one who harvests. It is just as essential to prepare the soil, to plant, and to water.

STAGES OF SPIRITUAL DEVELOPMENT

Below are eight major steps that I believe typify the process of spiritual development in most people: [3]

Awareness of God

⇓

Understanding of the basics of the Gospel

⇓

A positive attitude toward the Gospel

⇓

Personal problem recognition

⇓

Repentance and faith/commitment

⇓

Fellowship with other Christians

⇓

Change in behavior and attitude

⇓

Sharing faith [4]

It's true that leading someone to make a commitment to Christ shouldn't be done too hastily, before an individual is ready. However, that doesn't mean we can rely on our ability to properly diagnose whether someone is ready to become a Christian. What if we have only one shot with a kid? Do we forego helping someone make a faith commitment if we're not sure that person fully understands the message of Christ?

Terrance was such a teenager. He attended one of our detention center Bible studies, and his heart was definitely moved by what was said. At the close of the meeting, we offered teenagers the opportunity to make a commitment to Christ by inviting them to pray along with us. Terrance told us, as we were leaving, that he had prayed with us. We never saw Terrance again. And as time passed, we forgot about him.

Nearly two years later, we received a call from a friend of ours who was working as a counselor in another juvenile jail. She told us Terrance was in her office and he wanted to speak to us.

"Do you remember me?" he asked. "I prayed with you guys to become a Christian a long time ago. I've been reading my Bible ever since. I just got transferred to this new program, and I asked if there were any Christians here. They told me about Carol. After I told her how I had asked Jesus to be a part of my life when I was in your Bible study, she asked me if I wanted to call you." God was faithful to grow Terrance even when no one else was there to disciple him.

There have been many who had no prior knowledge of God or of the good news of Jesus, yet in a moment were gripped by the Holy Spirit through preaching or someone's sharing. They then repented of their sin, made a commitment to Christ, and instantly began growing in their faith. If we assume that the hearer must know and embrace all the basics of the Christian faith before making a legitimate commitment to Christ, we wrongly place ourselves in the role of the Holy Spirit.

Yet most of us have experienced the discouragement of seeing teenagers believe in Jesus and get all excited about the Lord, only to seemingly die on the vine. I remember a particularly discouraging point in our ministry. After having seen hundreds of incarcerated teenagers make commitments to Jesus but only a handful really living for Christ, I had concluded that one of three realities must be true: (1) These youth were so damaged, hardened, and far removed from anything remotely Christian that they were unable to fully embrace and trust God; (2) God, because of his decision to grant free will, was unable to really change them; or (3) we were doing something wrong.

Since it would be unorthodox to conclude one of the first two, I settled on number three. What were we doing wrong? How could we be more effective in our evangelism efforts with at-risk youth? There are no quick and easy solutions to these questions, but we'll revisit the struggle in more depth in chapters 10 and 11.

THE PARABLE OF THE SOWER

The parable of the sower in Luke 8:5-15 provides some insight into what often happens when a person is led into making a faith commitment prematurely. A young person who has an awareness of God but no understanding of the basics of the Gospel of Jesus Christ can be like "Those along the path...who hear, [but] then the devil comes and takes away the word from their hearts, so that they may not believe and be saved" (Luke 8:12).

Someone who has an understanding of the basics of the Gospel but hasn't begun to internalize it can be like "Those on the rock...who receive the word with joy when they hear it, but they have no root. They believe for a while, but in the time of testing they fall away" (Luke 8:13).

Likewise, those who possess a positive attitude toward the Gospel but haven't yet reached a place of brokenness or haven't felt need resemble "The seed that fell among thorns...as they go on their way they are choked by life's worries, riches and pleasures, and they do not mature" (Luke 8:14).

But when people's hearts have been made ready for the Gospel, they're like the "good soil...[they] hear the word, retain it, and by persevering produce a crop" (Luke 8:15). The chart below illustrates this process:

Awareness of God ⇓ Understanding of the basics of the Gospel ⇓ A positive attitude toward the Gospel ⇓ Personal problem recognition ⇓ Repentance and faith/commitment ⇓ Fellowship with other Christians ⇓ Change in behavior and attitude ⇓ Sharing faith [4]

Path (Luke 8:5-15) ⇓ Rocky ground ⇓ Thorns ⇓ Good soil ⇓

A MINISTRY STRATEGY

Bearing in mind these stages, notice how the Apostle John laid out a practical ministry strategy in 1 John 1:1: "That which was from the begin-ning, which we have *heard,* which we have *seen* with our eyes, which we have looked at and our hands have *touched*—this we *proclaim* concerning the Word of life" (author's emphasis).

Troubled teenagers need to hear, see, and touch the Gospel through our lives. They usually need to test it before they're ready to have it proclaimed to them. Scripture clearly illustrates this principle in the account of the woman at the well: "Many of the Samaritans...believed in [Jesus] because of the [Samaritan] woman's testimony." But after being with Jesus for a while, they began to shift the source of their belief, saying, "We no longer believe just because of what you said; now we have heard for ourselves, and we know that this man really is the Savior of the world" (John 4:39, 42).

1 John 1:1-3 illustrates how this process becomes more and more incarnational—people representing Jesus and pointing others to him—as a young person moves along the continuum.

Awareness of God	Heard (1 John 1:1)
⇓	⇓
Understanding of the basics of the Gospel	Seen
⇓	⇓
A positive attitude toward the Gospel	Touched
⇓	⇓
Personal problem recognition	Proclaimed
⇓	⇓
Repentance and faith/commitment	Have fellowship (Verse 3)
⇓	⇓
Fellowship with other Christians	
⇓	
Change in behavior and attitude	
⇓	
Sharing faith [4]	

Sharing the Gospel verbally—so someone *hears* the message—repre-sents the least involvement from the one sharing Christ. It's much more personal to show your faith—so another person can *see* it lived out in your life. But to allow someone to *touch* and be touched by your life is even more impacting. When a young person has the opportunity to experience this process, by the time the message is finally *proclaimed,* the chances are much better that he or she will be ready to respond with authentic faith.

This process doesn't end with the faith commitment, however. Once someone has become a Christian, 1 John 1:3 offers a strategy for the completion of evangelism: "We proclaim to you what we have seen and heard, so that you also may have *fellowship* with us. And our fellowship is with the Father and with his Son, Jesus Christ" (author's emphasis). We'll talk much more about this essential issue, fellowship, in chapter 6.

Assessing—Ten Years Later

Most of what we do in youth ministry doesn't bear immediate fruit. That's why it's helpful to think more in terms of our investment bearing fruit five to ten years beyond the teenage years.

In the movie *City Slickers,* Billy Crystal's character asks his two best friends—all three of them are in midlife crisis—two probing questions: "What was the best day of your life?" and "What was the worst day of your life?" Interestingly, most of the responses they gave dated back to when they were kids.

I once attended a men's retreat where we were presented with the same questions. In the context of a small group, each of us relayed to the others "the best day of my life" and "the worst day of my life." Nearly every one of us described incidents from our childhood or teenage years.

Recalling his worst day, one man told how at age ten he had gone to the neighborhood ice rink to play hockey. "As they started picking teams, it ultimately came down to me and one other kid for the last pick. He was chosen over me. Then as the other captain eyed me, he said, 'We'll go with a player short.' He turned around and walked away."

With a lump in his throat, he confessed, "I'm thirty-eight years old now, and that's the last time I ever played organized sports."

Although most people tend to rack up the worst days of their lives while they're teenagers, we also have the opportunity to give young people the best days of their lives. Having been in youth ministry for many years, I've seen the profound impact of some of those "best days."

It usually begins a year or two after teenagers graduate from college. They have pursued their dreams, gotten their first jobs, and now are beginning to feel somewhat disillusioned with where it all has gotten them. Typically, their faith has taken a back seat to grand visions. But now, somehow their dreams haven't delivered all they promised, so young people begin to reflect and ask, "What was the best day of my life?" "What really got me excited?"

It's at this point that I've received phone calls from some who were part of our youth group years earlier: "Scott, do you remember when I was in youth group and you took us into that prison to minister?" or "Remember when we used to feed the homeless in Boston?" or "You know, I've been thinking about how we used to go into that nursing home and sing and talk to the people."

The conversation often ends with something like this: "Meeting those people and seeing God use me was probably the best thing that's ever happened to me. Do you think I could get involved in doing something like that again?"

Recently I was with one of the first boys who lived with us. He had fallen a long way since leaving, and he was just starting to make his way back. During our conversation he told me, "In those two years I spent at the house I experienced more things than the rest of my life combined—far more than anybody else I know on the streets. Even while I'd been doing bad, I couldn't forget about what I had experienced through those mission trips and youth retreats. It used to haunt me day and night to know what I was missing. I finally couldn't keep buying the lie that sin was fun and following God was boring. It was those memories that eventually drove me back to God again."

No matter what happens after an authentic encounter with Christ, a teenager never can completely deny that God is real. Instead, he or she can say as Job did, "My ears had heard of you but now my eyes have seen you" (Job 42:5).

Environments Where Youth Encounter Christ

Camps and retreats offer tremendous potential for youth to encounter Christ. They're removed from their normal environment and exposed to God's presence in an intensified setting. Several of "the best days of my life" happened at youth camps, which is why I continue to speak at several each year. I've seen God completely alter the course of a young person's life in less than forty-eight hours on a weekend retreat. Of course, altering the course doesn't mean an instant makeover. But for many, it represents the beginning of an entirely new direction for their lives.

Mission trips often are even more impacting than retreats. I remember listening to the young people at our church describe their summer mission trip. "God was really there! I've been going to church all my life, but this was the first time I knew God was really real!"

These events are difficult to pull off, especially when you're working with troubled teenagers. Hanne used to take inner-city youth on summer canoe trips into the boundary waters of Minnesota and Canada. She would work for months to raise the money, recruit and prepare young people for the trip, and make arrangements for transportation and supplies.

Inevitably, on the morning of departure, when she went to pick up the girls, at least half of them were nowhere to be found. At the last minute, she would find others to bring instead. That was always one of the "worst days of her life." But once there, all the hard work of preparation and the sleepless nights soon faded in comparison to the eternal results manifested in the lives of young people.

Summary

We've been discussing the necessity for young people to experience a personal and genuine encounter with Jesus Christ.

A genuine encounter with Christ...

Is Not • **merely an emotional experience**—While emotions are an important component of who we are, decisions made purely on the basis of emotions seldom last. We shouldn't belittle the role of emotions, for often they're the windows through which some of the most effective ministry can happen. Yet if we aren't careful, we can use them to manipulate teenagers into making decisions prematurely. And because emotions change continuously, we don't want to teach teenagers to rely on them as a basis for decision-making.

Is Not • **the same experience for everyone**—We all have encountered Christ in different ways. God has met each of us uniquely, at key junctures in our lives. Perhaps that's why Jesus never approached two people in exactly the same way. He met each one right where that person was and got quickly to the core issues in the person's life.

Because we've powerfully encountered Christ, it's natural for us to want to give teenagers that same experience. Certainly it can be helpful to tell our own stories to teenagers. But to try to orchestrate the same experiences for them only causes frustration for them and us. We need to trust that God is working just as actively and uniquely in the lives of these young people as he is in our own lives. And while we will want to do all we can to create opportunities for teenagers to encounter Christ, we shouldn't be disappointed if it doesn't happen in the way we would prefer.

For example, one of the boys in our home had attended many camps and moving church services, but the most convincing encounter he had with Christ was while sitting in his car about to go to work. "God's presence just filled my car!" he later exclaimed. "I felt like God was telling me how much he loved me and that he had a purpose for my life. I never wear a seat belt when I drive, mostly because I never felt my life was worth saving. But that morning, I even put my seat belt on. It was sort of a way of saying, 'My life is valuable and worth something.' It was awesome! Come out and sit in my car. Put the seat belt on. You'll feel it!" God had met him in his own unique way.

IS NOT • **the end product or final goal**—Christian maturity consists of far more than just an isolated spiritual experience. Without a discipleship relationship with a more mature Christian and getting grounded in a local church, few ever mature beyond a few isolated encounters with Christ.

A genuine encounter with Christ...

IS • **essential**—There's no such thing as a "second-generation Christian." Even for those reared in solid Christian homes, each person must come to a point where he or she sees an individual need for Christ—where that person can cry out to God and experience meeting God in a personal way. It's to this end that we must pray for God's intervention in the lives of the young people we encounter.

We must also work to create settings where Christ can break through and touch young people. Retreats, mission trips, and service projects all can provide an environment for such an experience. The extra work and energy involved in pulling off such activities is always worth the investment.

If young people need such an encounter, we need it just as much. How are you and your leadership staff encountering Christ in fresh ways? None of us can live off yesterday's experiences.

IS • **a process**—While spiritual birth may be a specific act that happens at a moment in time, there is a process that both precedes and follows that event. If we see evangelism as a continuum, we can then recognize spiritual growth at every point in the continuum.

The more young people have the opportunity to hear, see, and touch the message through us—the messengers—the better chance their decisions have of ultimately bearing fruit. Without the soil being properly readied and the seed being sown, watered, and nurtured, a ripened harvest is unlikely.

IS • **something only God can do**—Although we can work diligently to create an environment in which youth can genuinely encounter Christ, we can't make it happen. A real faith commitment is a miracle that only God can make happen. Apart from the work of the Holy Spirit, nothing truly spiritual can result (John 14:6, 15:5).

The Apostle Paul was mindful of this when he declared, "My message and my preaching were not with wise and persuasive words, but with a demonstration of the Spirit's power, so that your faith might not rest on men's wisdom, but on God's power" (1 Corinthians 2:4-5).

How is that power released? Largely through prayer. I've seen over and over how little fruit my efforts often produce and how much concerted prayer actually can accomplish. While I always have believed this, I still find myself devoting tons of energy into trying to change teenagers and relatively little energy into prayer by comparison.

Hanne and I had been talking with Matt for months about a particular issue he was struggling with and his need to surrender every area of his life to Christ. He was hearing us, but it just wasn't connecting for him. Finally out of frustration we decided to quit talking to him about it and committed to fervent prayer about the matter.

Within a week, Matt came to us with a decision he had made. "I've decided that I really need to give this area of my life over to God. I know that my main focus needs to be God if I'm ever going to really make it."

When will we ever learn? Ephesians 6:12 tells us that our struggle isn't against flesh and blood. Spiritual battles must be fought in a spiritual manner, and as James says, "The effective, fervent prayer of a righteous man avails much" (James 5:16b, New King James Version).

ENDNOTES

1. Gordon McLean, telephone interview, Chicago, IL, January 30, 1996.

2. Francis A. Schaeffer, *The God Who Is There,* (Chicago, IL: Inter-Varsity Press, 1968), 143.

3. Scott Larson, Dave Van Patten, and Alexander Dunlop, with funding from Prison Fellowship, developed *Quick Connect,* which outlines these steps in more detail. The survey will be published by Group Publishing in 2000.

4. These categories were derived largely from James Engel's "Spiritual-Decision Process," which actually contains fifteen stages as outlined in *What's Gone Wrong With the Harvest?: A Communication Strategy for the Church and World Evangelization* (Grand Rapids, MI: Zondervan Publishing House, 1975), 45.

YOUTH MINISTRY EVALUATION

Providing a Genuine Encounter With Christ

Rate your youth ministry in each of the following areas by circling the appropriate number.

1	2	3	4	5
We don't think much about providing teenagers with opportunities to encounter Christ.			We're very intentional about creating environments for teenagers to authentically encounter Christ.	

1	2	3	4	5
We don't have any specific prayer focus for our teenagers outside youth meetings.			We have a prayer network so each of our young people is prayed for on a regular basis.	

1	2	3	4	5
We don't tend to focus much on pre-evangelism.			We focus on pre-evangelism as much as we do evangelism.	

1	2	3	4	5
Our program is weak on follow-up with teenagers who make commitments to Christ.			Our program is strong on follow-up and discipleship for new Christians.	

1	2	3	4	5
We tend to stay away from doctrine and theological teaching with our teenagers.			We have a rotation so that every teenager in our program learns the basic doctrines of the Christian faith.	

Total score: _____ (Enter this score in the scoring key on page 132.)

CHAPTER 5:
A New Identity in Christ

*Because I have become accustomed to failure,
I tend to fear success. Therefore I need to see
myself as God sees me so I can live in accordance
with that identity.*

Formerly he was useless to you, but now he has become useful both to you and to me (Philemon 11).

If ever there was a segment of our population with an identity crisis, it's troubled teenagers. I once asked the group of young people at a detention center Bible study, "What would you like to be doing in five years?"

While others were still pondering, Luis didn't hesitate at all. "I'll be in prison in five years."

"Why do you say that?" I challenged him. "You'll be out of here in a couple of months."

"'Cause I've always *been* a troublemaker, and I'll always *be* a troublemaker."

I wondered how many times Luis had heard that said about himself. Contrast that with Onesimus, of whom Paul said, "He has become useful both to you and to me," Luis had heard only how useless he was, so much so that he now owned it as part of his own identity.

Failure Complex

Most at-risk youth have experienced so much failure in their young lives that they no longer believe they can succeed at anything. In fact, many of them subtly begin to feel more comfortable failing than they do succeeding. Success is scary. Failure is at least familiar.

This was the case with Steve. One day we went with him to his room after the detention center Bible study and discovered that he had a real gift for art. He could see we were particularly impressed by one of the paintings he had made.

"Do you want that one?" he asked.

"Oh, that would be great, Steve."

As I reached out to take it, he informed me that we couldn't have it just yet. He said he wasn't finished with it.

"Really? What do you have left to do?" we asked.

"Oh, I haven't signed it yet. I'll give it to you next week."

Several weeks went by. Each time we asked if he had signed the painting yet, his response was always the same: "No, not yet. But I'll give it to you as soon as I'm finished."

It finally dawned on us why Steve might be so hesitant to complete the painting. As long as his work wasn't finished, nobody could criticize it. But once it was completed, his painting was open for inspection, something that posed the possibility of failure.

Over and over, we've seen teenagers fail or get kicked out of programs just days before graduation. Why? For many of them, successfully completing something places great pressure on them. If people suddenly start believing in them, they'll be expected to continue to succeed. This is a paralyzing thought for someone who feels incapable or unworthy of success. And in the eyes of many, newfound success would likely be short-lived anyway. They see it as merely a setup for an even greater fall in the future.

Not long ago, we saw Billy back in the detention center where we had seen him many times over the past three years. "What happened, Billy?"

"I don't know. I guess I was just doing *too* good," he responded.

"*Too* good? That's a new one. People don't usually end up back in here for doing too good," I countered.

"Well, I was back in school, I had a job, and things were really coming together. My family was proud of me—for the first time I can remember. Then I just started getting scared. I knew I wouldn't be able to keep it up, and eventually I was going to crash and disappoint everybody. So I figured I might as well just screw up now, before I had too much to lose."

Failure complexes run so deep. It's not surprising that one of the most common tattoos worn in adult prisons is the phrase "Born to Lose."

What is the source of this failure complex resident in so many troubled teenagers? And how does that affect their sense of identity? For many, fatherlessness is at the core.

A Father's Influence on Identity

Dr. David Popenoe, professor of sociology at Rutgers University, explains some of what fathers provide: "Adult male role models are especially important for controlling the behavior of teenage boys. The discipline and authority that men bring to raising boys are very difficult for a woman alone to achieve. Without adult males around, teenage boys will necessarily turn excessively to their peers and to the antisocial behavior that male teenage peer groups often engender...

"The pathway to adulthood for daughters is somewhat easier than it is for sons...but they still must learn from their fathers, as they cannot from their mothers, how to relate to men. They learn from their fathers about heterosexual trust, intimacy, and [the] difference [between the sexes]. They learn to appreciate their own femininity from the one male who is most special in their lives... Most importantly, through loving and being loved by their fathers, they learn that they are love-worthy." [1]

Does that eliminate hope for those who are beyond the formative years and never have had a positive adult male influence? No. God is in the business of redeeming and rebuilding broken lives. But that process often requires someone to take on that fatherly role in the person's life, especially for boys.

THE POWER OF NEIGHBORING

We lived in a small town in Minnesota until I was ten years old. Unlike most neighborhoods today, ours was one where fences didn't separate the backyards of neighbors. During the summer, it was typical for every family on the block to congregate in one backyard for dinner one or two nights a week. Mothers were mothers to all the kids on the block. Fathers served as fathers to all the kids. It wasn't uncommon for a family to invite other neighborhood kids with them on family vacations.

I remember our neighbor Mr. Noetzel, the high school wrestling coach, who regularly took his son and me to wrestling practices with him. There was something powerful about being with those high school "giants." Just hanging around Mr. Noetzel and those young men made an indelible impression upon me as a seven-year-old boy. I was beginning to gain a sense of manhood.

A few years later we moved to a farm, where hunting trips provided something similar for me. In fact, in my early teens I experienced one of the most significant days of my life. It happened the day my father felt I was finally ready to participate in the "big annual hunt." This wasn't for little kids, you see, and you could go only when your father had determined you were ready.

Excitement made it hard to sleep the night before. But at 4 a.m. on the opening day of hunting season, fathers and sons everywhere got up, put on bright orange clothes, and congregated at one end of a newly harvested corn-field. With the sun not yet poking over the horizon and steam rising from our bodies, thirty or so men and boys, with shotguns loaded, prepared to begin the pursuit of the sought-after prize—a three-pound pheasant. While it may seem a bit silly, there was something very powerful about that day for me. And although I'm not a hunter today, that culturally relevant experience somehow served as a sort of rite of passage to manhood for me.

Contrast that with Tyrone, a thirteen-year-old boy who attended one of our Bible studies. His feet could barely touch the ground as he sat on his chair. He was telling me, with great animation, about how he had pinned another shaking kid to the ground.

"I held a gun to his head and told him, 'I got the power to take your life or to give it back to you...I'm gonna let you live.'" My assumptions about him were right. As I inquired, I learned that Tyrone had never received any positive male influence in his life. He had no idea who he was or what it meant to be a man.

While a mother does many essential things, one thing she can't do is model for a boy how to be a man. A Los Angeles Times Magazine cover story entitled "Mothers, Sons, and the Gangs" featured the writer interviewing several single mothers who each lamented, "I don't understand why my boy hangs out on the streets. I'm a good mother. I keep a clean house. I go to church. I don't run around with men. I cook for the boy, wash his clothes, and provide a good home. Why doesn't he want to stay here?" [2]

Research has shown clearly that when a good father influence is lacking, boys lack a healthy understanding of what male identity is. So they tend to act out very exaggerated notions of masculinity, including extreme aggression, sexual promiscuity, and physical abuse of women. [3] The father's influence is what usually gives both sons and daughters a healthy sense of self-confidence, counteracting the destructive failure complex that often surfaces in his absence. [4]

One of the disturbing things I've observed in working with hundreds of juvenile offenders is that at least one out of four already have children of their own. Tragically, at such a young age, they're already passing on the same "disease" that was passed on to them: Virtually none of them are actively involved in the lives of their own children.

Scripture makes a very clear distinction between *fathering* and *begetting*. The Biblical genealogies say, "So and so begat so and so; who begat so and so..." *Begetting* is simply the act of impregnating a woman who then conceives a child. It has nothing to do with *fathering*. Fathering is altogether different. And the fact that one of God's titles is "Father" gives us an even greater understanding of what fatherhood entails.

How Views of God as Father Affect Identity

I believe it was C. S. Lewis who said that at creation God made us in his image and we've been working ever since to return the favor. Rather than seeing ourselves as bearers of the image of God, we instead tend to view God through the lens of our own image. This is particularly true when it comes to how we define God as Father.

We have seen over and over how profoundly the definition we hold of our earthly father influences our view of our Heavenly Father. While God sometimes refers to himself as a shepherd, sometimes as a king, sometimes as a counselor, even at times a spouse, the most common title God uses for self-description is "Father." This makes the role of our earthly fathers all the more significant, for it so strongly influences how we come to understand and relate to God.

Over the years, I've observed five general types of fathers: abusive fathers, absent fathers, passive fathers, performance-based fathers, and loving fathers. [5]

ABUSIVE FATHERS

I once asked young people in a detention center how many had experienced rejection while growing up. Out of twelve young people in the group, five relayed stories of how a father or stepfather had tried to seriously hurt them when they were young. Is it any surprise that these boys might have difficulty trusting a Heavenly Father?

Both my parents grew up with abusive fathers. By God's grace they were able to overcome those issues, find healing from that damage, and avoid passing it on to any of their children. Fortunately our family witnessed the breaking of the curse spoken of in Deuteronomy 5:9b: "visiting the iniquity of the fathers upon the children to the third and fourth generation" (King James Version). Instead God helped my parents begin the cycle of "showing steadfast love to thousands of those who love me and keep my commandments" (Deuteronomy 5:10, Revised Standard Edition).

If God uses us to help teenagers break the chain of abuse in their own backgrounds, we affect not only them but generations to come.

ABSENT FATHERS

Though the vast majority of troubled teenagers grow up in homes where fathers aren't present, this is not the only condition of absent fatherhood. A father can live at the same address as his children but reside in an altogether different world.

A well-known Christian leader brought together a group of younger leaders to invest some of his wisdom and experience into our lives. One of the most significant things he offered us was the opportunity to ask questions of his grown children about what it was like living with such a high-profile father.

Somebody inquired of his youngest son, "What is your view of God?" After thinking rather carefully, he responded, "I guess I tend to think of God as being somewhere over in Australia taking care of more important things."

While dad might be physically present, when he's obviously consumed with other matters, teenagers can develop a "Bette Midler" theology, expressed in her hit song from the 1980s: "God is watching us from a distance."

PASSIVE FATHERS

Many fathers have abdicated the role of child-rearing to the mother. They are passively involved in the lives of their children. Rather than sharing the responsibility of disciplining, nurturing, and teaching, their response to their children's questions is "Go ask your mother." Their children seldom see them involved in the daily decisions that affect the family—except the big ones, like moving the family to another state because of a job promotion.

This type of father role is detrimental to a child's understanding of family and produces a warped image of God as well. Children of passive fathers tend to develop a similar view of God. They see God as a nice old man in a rocking chair. For while God may be remotely concerned with their affairs, when push comes to shove, if anything's going to get done, they know they're going to have to be the ones to do it.

PERFORMANCE-BASED FATHERS

I was speaking at a high school camp when sixteen-year-old Ricky came up to me after the first session and said, "I just hope you're not going down a path where at the end of the weekend you're going to ask us to 'rededicate' our lives to God and commit to serving him with our whole heart. 'Cause if you are, I want to go home right now.

"I've been coming here for a long time, and I've made these promises year after year, promises I can never keep, and then I end up worse off than before I started, with God even more mad at me. 'Cause now, not only am I sinning, but I'm breaking another promise I made to God. And so I just want to make sure that's not where you're headed this weekend. Is it?"

It was then that Ricky took his first breath, allowing me to respond. His question took me by surprise. Not only was I potentially going to have to change my whole agenda for the weekend, but more importantly I felt really sad for all the frustration he was feeling. Not knowing what to say, I decided to ask him a question instead. "What can you tell me about your dad, Ricky?"

Appearing equally stunned by my question, he proceeded to tell me a story from when he was in about the sixth grade. "Every day when my dad would come home from work, the first thing he would always ask me was, 'Have you done your homework yet?' It was always a pretty safe bet that I hadn't.

"Then one day I decided to surprise him. When he got home, I met him at the door saying, 'Guess what, dad, I did all my homework!'

"His response was, 'Then why aren't you working on tomorrow's?' "

Suddenly I wasn't so surprised Ricky felt the way he did about himself and about God. He had learned that he could never make the mark. And as soon as he started even getting close to it, the mark would always move up a few notches higher, further confirming the fact that he would always come up short.

This is a destructive image of fatherhood, one that's a long way from the truth of what our Heavenly Father personifies.

LOVING FATHERS

One of the best illustrations of who God as Father really is was told by Jesus in Luke 15:11-32 in the parable we've come to know as "The Prodigal Son." Perhaps it might better be titled "The Loving Father."

Rather than giving an "I told you so" lecture, the father ran down the road to meet his wayward son—the very one who had squandered half his assets and in the process cut his earning ability in half; the one who had squandered all that hard-earned money on sex and wild parties; the one who had then completely disappeared, leaving without so much as a "thank you"; the one who hadn't kept in touch at all, until now, when there was nowhere else to turn.

It was this one the father ran out to meet, threw his arms around, and kissed. Filled with compassion, he ordered his servants to bring the best robe, to put a ring on his finger and sandals on his feet, and then to bring the fattened calf and kill it. He saw it as a cause for celebration: His son who had been lost was now found!

In which of these categories would you place your earthly father? How has that influenced your view of God as our Heavenly Father? If you're a father, into which category do you fit when it comes to dealing with your children? Take some time to think and pray about that. Your answer affects how you'll tend to view the young people you're ministering to and how they'll come to view you—and perhaps God as well.

Once we begin to have a more accurate picture of who God is, we then need to understand more clearly who we are as God's *daughters* and *sons*. When young people begin to grasp what it means to be full-fledged children of God, their actions and ways of thinking will start to change. But to fully embrace the lifestyle of a son or daughter in Christ, young people must first leave behind the orphan lifestyle into which they were born, something more easily said than done.

The Orphan Lifestyle

When Jim and Susan found out they weren't able to have children, they were devastated by the news. But eventually they began to get excited about the possibility of adopting a needy child from a developing country. They soon discovered it wouldn't be an easy task. The amount of money and red tape involved in the application process was only half the battle. After that came the long wait.

It was nearly two years before they received the wonderful news: They would be getting a five-year-old little girl from Calcutta, India! They were ecstatic and almost immediately began the work of renovating a spare bedroom into a little girl's dream.

Jim was a carpenter and did all the work. No expense was spared: hand-made furniture, new wallpaper and carpeting, a play area. The room was overflowing with new baby dolls and stuffed animals. The final touch was a canopy over the bed that matched the curtains.

The project was finished just in time for the grand arrival of their new little daughter, Maria. Before going to the airport, they set the table with their finest china and prepared a feast for their first dinner together as a family.

Of course they couldn't communicate with their new little girl, as they didn't speak the same language. But the smiles they exchanged on the ride home more than sufficed.

When they arrived at the house, little Maria was shown her room. Then, before dinner, Jim and Susan took off her old clothes and put on the brand new dress they had bought for her. It was at the dinner table that they began to notice some of Maria's strange behavior. Whenever she thought no one was looking, she would take dinner rolls from the table and stuff them under her dress. Though they tried to explain that she could have all she wanted, that everything in the house was hers, the message wasn't sinking in.

That evening, they put on her new pajamas and tucked her into bed. Checking on her an hour later, they were surprised to find little Maria curled up in a corner of the bedroom. She had put her old clothes back on and was eating the rolls she had taken from the table. Even though Maria had been changed from an orphan into a full-fledged daughter almost instantaneously, it would take much longer for the orphan mind-set to leave this little girl.

Galatians 4:1-7 illustrates how we, as children of God, have been changed from orphans to full-fledged sons and daughters of the King. Satan can't do a thing about that reality. What Satan can do, though, is try to make us feel and act like orphans again—in essence, negating the benefits we've been granted as heirs of our Heavenly Father.

Most troubled teenagers have fully embodied the lifestyle of an orphan. Orphans believe they must steal, for they know that nobody else is going to take care of them. Orphans have to lie and cheat to get ahead, since no one else will advocate for them. They must boast and brag to build themselves up in the eyes of others, for if anyone knew what they're really like, people would have nothing to do with them.

Orphans gossip, trying to build themselves up by tearing others down. Orphans live in fear, as they have no sense that anyone else is concerned with protecting them. They're insecure, always focusing on themselves, for who else would ever care enough about them to pay them any attention?

When young people like this make commitments to Christ, they're instantly made into full-fledged sons and daughters of God. But just like little Maria, the orphan mind-set takes much longer to shed. Many, in fact, never break out of it.

How can we help young people shed this orphan complex and begin walking as full-fledged children of God? Simply telling a young person, "You can do it" or "Believe in yourself" is grossly inadequate. The power of positive thinking just isn't enough. Most of these young people are well aware of their faults. They have a pretty good sense of what their lives are about, and it's not a pretty picture.

A New Identity in Christ

Fortunately God doesn't use a simplistic "I'm OK, you're OK" approach. God's approach is far more radical than that. When we surrender our lives to

God, our old selves are put to death. Then God resurrects us anew in Christ.

In 2 Corinthians 5:17 Paul says, "If anyone is in Christ, he is a new creation; the old has gone, the new has come!" That term "new creation" implies the birth of an entirely new being, one that never before existed. God replaces an old self with a completely new one, one in which identity is now rooted in God's very nature!

Young people can't really change until they know their true identity in Christ, this secure position they now possess. This is a process; it doesn't happen overnight. But it must be the crux of how we disciple young believers. For that is ultimately what will begin to change their daily actions and lifestyle.

RICKY

Ricky pulled us aside after a detention center Bible study. He informed us that he secretly had been making weapons in his room. He was constructing them out of combs and plastic silverware and hiding them under his bed.

When we asked him how he felt about that, he said, "I feel bad. That's why I wanted to talk with you. I'm not even sure why I'm doing it. I guess it's just a habit or something."

"Ricky, you feel bad because God has made you a new person. The old Ricky would have felt very comfortable making and using weapons. But that old person doesn't exist anymore. God has made you into a new person."

His face began to light up as we talked. Soon we all had to line up for dinner. When Ricky came into line a few minutes later, he whispered to us that he had just thrown away all his weapons.

FOR AS HE THINKS WITHIN HIMSELF, SO HE IS (PROVERBS 23:7, NASB)

A common mistake many ministries have made, ours included, is to put teenagers on stage to share their stories prematurely, before they're grounded in an understanding of their identity in Christ. This is tempting to do, for invariably listeners are more than a little impressed. "Wow, look at how this kid has changed. His life was once wracked with drugs, crime, abuse, and prison—and now he's a strong Christian!" Not only does it build the faith of the listener, but it also can be a really effective fund-raiser for the ministry that is putting the teenager on display.

The problem surfaces, however, when after the meeting, people line up to tell the young Christian how wonderful he or she is, how the sharing was one of the most powerful things they've ever heard. Of course, it's important to compliment and build up young people. But what often happens in these situations is that the young person is put on a pedestal, one the person knows he or she will fall off. The teenager is being called a perfect "ten" but he still sees himself or herself as a "two."

This disparity can't last for long. Whether consciously or subconsciously, a teenager will almost invariably do something to mess up, something bad enough to bring others' expectations back down to the "two" level, where he or she feels more comfortable, where the territory is more familiar.

RONALD

One Sunday morning when I was speaking at a church service, I brought four of the guys from our home with me. During the service, the pastor unexpectedly said, "Before Scott comes to bring this morning's message, we would like to hear from one of the boys he has with him about how God has changed his life." All of the guys who were with me that day had lived with us for only a short time. None of them were ready to publicly share their stories in a church service.

Yet after hearing what the pastor was expecting, I leaned over to the boy next to me and asked if he would be willing to share. He looked very frightened and quickly gestured "no." I went down the line, asking each one the same question. None of them wanted to.

Finally I came to the last boy, Ronald. "Do I have to?" he asked.

"No, you don't have to. But would you be willing?" I pleaded.

Reluctantly he agreed. "Well, I guess so. But I don't really know what to say."

Ronald did a fantastic job. People were sincerely moved by what he had to say, even though, as is often the case with new Christians, most of his testimony focused on the bad things of the past rather than the good God was currently doing. This isn't hard to understand, since it's usually the bad stuff people are most interested in hearing anyway. It's much more exciting to hear the details of a past life of crime than of one's humble devotion to Christ.

On the way home Ronald remarked, "This has been the best day of my life. It's hard for me to believe how much things have changed in me."

We agreed. "We're so proud of you, Ronald. You've come so far."

By this time, Ronald had been living with us for three months. He had been doing reasonably well. He'd had a few minor bumps along the way, but nothing too major. In fact, just a few weeks before, he had seemed to really turn a major corner, believing for the first time he really could make it. That's when it often begins to get scary for many of these teenagers.

The very next morning when one of our associate staff members got into his car, he was confused. It seemed to be parked a little differently from where he remembered leaving it the night before. The radio and heater were also adjusted slightly differently. And upon further investigation, he noted an extra 150 miles on the car!

As we spoke to each of the guys, it became clear that Ronald had taken the car. He had gone into the staff person's bedroom at one o'clock in the morning and taken the keys while he was sleeping. Ronald drove around until four o'clock and then came back and went to bed.

During our confrontation, Hanne asked, "Ronald, is this about doing the worst thing you could think of, trying to get caught, and then testing us to see if we would still love you?" He began to cry and nodded. In the end, Ronald's view of himself was so low and inconsistent with the pedestal he was placed upon that it didn't take him long to knock himself back down to that more comfortable and familiar place.

OUR POSITION IN CHRIST MUST ALWAYS INFLUENCE OUR CONDITION

How do we help young people like Ronald move to a higher level in how they view their own identity? What do they need to be taught?

Careful examination of the Pauline Epistles reveals that Paul seldom told his readers what to do until he first explained to them who God was and who they were as God's children. Consider the fact that he spent the first eleven chapters of Romans largely explaining who these Roman believers were in Christ, before opening chapter 12 with "Therefore,...offer your bodies as living sacrifices." He then continued for the next four chapters, instructing the Romans in what they were to do.

Likewise, Paul spent most of the first three chapters of Ephesians detailing who God was and who the Ephesian believers were before charging them with what they should do, in the final three chapters. The first two chapters of Colossians speak mostly to our position as believers, while the last two emphasize the behavior that must follow. Philippians 1 primarily explains who we are, before the final three chapters instruct us on how to act. And Galatians presents four chapters on our identity in Christ before chapters 5 and 6 tell us what we must do as a response.

Watchman Nee illustrated this so well when he made the distinction between our *position* in Christ and the daily *condition* in which we find ourselves. [6] Our position never changes. Not only are we completely clean and void of sin when standing before a Holy God, but we also are completely righteous. The King James Version uses the term "imputed righteousness" in Romans 4:6. All the righteous works of Jesus have been imputed, or credited, into our account!

How does this happen? Paul explained in 2 Corinthians 5:21 that "God made him who had no sin to be sin for us, so that in him we might become the righteousness of God."

Most of us disciple people in just the opposite manner. We imply that if they do all the right things, then they'll be accepted by God. While we would never say it that way, this is often the message that gets communicated. How much time do we spend with new Christians, detailing the truths of who they are in Christ—fully accepted, forgiven, righteous, and holy before God—compared with how much time we spend telling them what they're supposed to do?

Many of us have sold the Gospel short, both in downplaying the depth of our sin and in downplaying the extent of our redemption. God didn't simply make us better than we were before we committed ourselves to Christ. God took our old sin nature and imputed it into the life of Jesus on the cross. This is the reason God the Father had to turn away, not even able to look upon Jesus on the cross (Mark 15:34). In that moment, God removed our sins, nailing them to the cross (Colossians 2:14), and put in their place all the righteousness of Christ.

Are these truths too deep for the new Christian? No. For this is the Gospel, the good news! Our position (that which never changes) should always be what influences our condition (that which tends to waver moment by moment).

If we don't teach these truths to new Christians, they often aren't receptive to them until much later when they eventually crash under the weight of trying to live the Christian life in their own strength. Let's not wait until then.

Summary

We've been discussing the need for youth to understand and begin to walk in their new identity as children of God.

This new identity...

IS NOT   • **pop psychology**—We aren't trying to psych teenagers into somehow believing they're better than they really are. On the contrary, unless they first understand the depth of their depravity, they cannot fully appreciate the extent of God's redemption.

IS NOT • **an excuse or denial of one's past**—We aren't trying to make excuses for the negative behaviors of teenagers. Each of us must take full responsibility for our past—our actions, attitudes, and faulty ways of thinking. Simply shifting the blame to society, family members, or others who may have failed us only serves to further enslave us. We can't embrace a new identity in Christ until we take full responsibility for who we are and what we've become.

IS NOT • **negating consequences for sinful actions**—Being forgiven doesn't nullify the earthly consequences for sinful actions. We still must pay consequences and make restitution. Yet our identity consists of more than just the worst things we've ever done. Society tends to label people according to their worst actions, calling them rapists, thieves, murderers, or liars, for example. But carrying such labels offers no power to change. In fact, it only further weakens people.

The Apostle Paul didn't deny his past. On several occasions he even referred to himself as "the chief of sinners." But even more, he opened nearly every letter by describing himself as "an apostle of Jesus Christ, by the will of God." The teenagers we work with need to develop that same attitude. Yes, they've messed up. And yes, there are consequences for that. But God has done the miraculous: God has turned that which was evil into something beautiful.

This new identity...

IS • **Scriptural**—God's Word must be the foundation for understanding these truths. They're spiritual, and therefore they can't be discerned apart from the Holy Spirit revealing them to us and the teenagers we work with. As we attempt to teach young people, we must use the Bible as our authority, not our own thoughts and ideas. God doesn't promise to honor our words, but God does say the Word won't return void (Isaiah 55:11). Not that simply putting God's Word before people is somehow magical. It must be communicated effectively, understood, and acted upon in order for it to change teenagers' lives.

Of course we can't help young people understand their identity in Christ if we don't understand it ourselves. Books like Hudson Taylor's *Spiritual Secret, The Normal Christian Life* by Watchman Nee, or *The Green Letters: Principles of Spiritual Growth* by Miles Stanford are good places to begin that process of understanding our new identity in Christ.

IS • **possible even when you're not allowed to share your faith openly**—Many Christians who work with at-risk teenagers in secular contexts aren't allowed to openly share their faith. In spite of that, the much-needed transference of a healthy identity still can be offered to teenagers. Schoolteachers, social workers, caseworkers, and clinicians all can have a powerful impact upon young people, just by their presence.

Many of the youth who have lived in our home were deeply touched by staff members at programs where they were placed. As staff, they were able to make powerful statements, even if they weren't allowed to articulate them with words.

In some cases, it was these relationships, as much as the clinical treatment they received, that laid the foundation for other trusting relationships. And after having the opportunity to *hear, see,* and *touch* the life of a committed Christian, these young people were better prepared to receive the message of Christ when it was later *proclaimed* to them (1 John 1:1).

• **something to be continually reinforced**—Most teenagers who have made it into the category of "at risk" have heard countless times that they're "no good," "full of trouble," and "unable to change." Thus, they'll need to hear this new message from the heart of God more than a few times, if it ever is to sink in.

Teenagers also need reinforcement when they do well, not just when they do poorly. One guy in jail told me, "It seems the only time I get any attention is when I get locked up. Then I have people who want to talk to me all day long—counselors, teachers, psychologists, even my parents. Everybody's suddenly very interested in me. And it feels good."

For this young man, doing crime was worth it if that's what it took to get attention. Unfortunately, the consequences for doing good don't come as quickly as do consequences for doing bad. We must work to change that. An old rule of thumb is "Kids need to hear seven positive statements about themselves for every negative one." If that's true, we have a great deal of catching up to do with these young people.

ENDNOTES

1. David Popenoe, *Life Without Father: Compelling New Evidence that Fatherhood and Marriage Are Indispensable for the Good of Children and Society* (New York: The Free Press, 1996), 142-143.

2. Sue Horton, "Mothers, Sons, and the Gangs: When a Gang Becomes Part of the Family," Los Angeles Times Magazine (October 16, 1988), 8.

3. Linda Nielson, *Adolescence: A Contemporary View,* 3rd Ed. (Fort Worth, TX: Harcourt Brace College Publishers, 1996), 309.

4. Nielson, *Adolescence: A Contemporary View,* 3rd Ed., 307-308.

5. The ideas for the first four of these categories were inspired by a talk given by Louie Gigglio at the Evangelistic Association of New England's Youth Workers Conference in Hopkinton, Massachusetts, April 1994.

6. Watchman Nee, *The Normal Christian Life* (Wheaton, IL: Tyndale House Publishers, Inc., 1985), 31-33.

YOUTH MINISTRY EVALUATION
Discipling Youth in Their New Identity in Christ

Rate your youth ministry in each of the following areas by circling the appropriate number.

1   **2**   **3**   **4**   **5**

With our teenagers, we tend to focus mostly on how they should behave.

We try to focus on who we are in Christ along with behavior issues.

1   **2**   **3**   **4**   **5**

We have a shortage of significant adult males involved with our youth.

We have a good balance of fatherly-type men ministering to our teenagers along with women.

1   **2**   **3**   **4**   **5**

Teenagers seem to get the most attention when they do bad things.

Teenagers receive more positive reinforcement than negative.

1   **2**   **3**   **4**   **5**

We don't have a discipleship program that emphasizes who we are in Christ for both our youth and our adults.

We have a discipleship program that emphasizes who we are in Christ for both our youth and our adults.

1   **2**   **3**   **4**   **5**

Sometimes we have teenagers share their stories before they're ready.

We don't allow teenagers to share their stories before they're ready.

Total score: _____ (Enter this score in the scoring key on page 132.)

CHAPTER 6:
A Place to Belong

Because I have experienced significant pain, I tend to not trust anybody. Therefore I need to feel I belong so I can take risks to trust again.

I am sending him—who is my very heart—back to you (Philemon 12).

"I hate Christmas," Terrance interrupted as we were discussing its meaning at the detention center Bible study.

"Hate Christmas? Why would anyone hate Christmas?" I wondered. But from the tone of his voice I knew I was about to find out.

"When I was seven, me and my younger brother and sister went to Dad's house for Christmas. The state allowed us to leave our foster home so we could spend Christmas with him and his girlfriend.

"We were really happy, especially when we saw all the presents under the tree. Tommy and Teesha kept trying to open them right away. But I told them we had to wait until Christmas morning. That's the way Dad did it.

"We couldn't sleep all night, wondering what was in those presents. We were the first ones to wake up. When everyone else finally woke up, my father's girlfriend took the presents one by one and gave them to her kids. We watched them open every present. None of them were for us.

"I could live with it. He already had let me down so many times that I didn't really expect anything different. But why did he have to do this to Tommy and Teesha? They still didn't know any better. I guess Christmas and most every other good thing just weren't meant for us.

"Anyway, I hate Christmas."

Damaged Youth

There's no doubt that many teenagers today carry an enormous amount of hurt and pain. And it's not just teenagers in jail.

At the beginning of a high school retreat filled with middle-class teenagers from churches all over New England, I asked students to each write down one thing they wanted God to do in their lives during the weekend. Here's a sampling of some of their requests:

"To get rid of the moment with John when I was five years old."

"I want God to take away the pain and to put Jason away for a long time."

"I have a lot of peer pressure about my weight. In the world today you're expected to have the body of a model."

"I want God to heal the pain that I suffer from being raped by someone who I thought was a friend."

"I was beaten as a child, and so the government took me and my sister away from them. I was adopted and I'm feeling like it was my fault. I don't know what to do."

"Help me to forgive and forget what my father has done to me and no more bad dreams."

"All I want is a dad."

Once while Hanne was leading a Bible study in a detention center on the topic of love, one of the girls interrupted, "There's only one I can really trust, who will never let me down. There's only one I can talk to about anything."

"Who's that, Tanya?" Hanne asked. "Your boyfriend?"

"No," she said, looking down, "my cat."

The Effects of Hurt

I often ask young people, "If you could go back to any point in your life and start over, how far back would you go?" It's amazing how quickly most can pinpoint a specific point in time, a pivotal event that put the person's life on a completely different course.

"I would go back to age twelve, when my father left home," said one boy.

"I'd go back to when I was nine. That's when my grandmother died and I quit caring about anything."

"When I was ten. That's when my father went to prison and my mother started doing drugs."

For many girls we see in jail, that pivotal moment came when their mother's live-in boyfriend began abusing them.

Hurts like these eventually make their way to the surface. Most of us only note the bizarre behaviors troubled teenagers exhibit; the real motives are often well disguised, hiding the real source of their actions.

LARRY

Larry went with our mentoring ministry on a whitewater rafting trip. We were surprised he had signed up, for all the way up to Maine he kept insisting he wasn't getting on any raft going down the river. After several hours we stopped trying to reason with him and just ignored his comments.

Even as we were carrying the raft down the path to the river, Larry still insisted he wasn't getting into the boat. Finally, left without any options, he hesitantly entered the raft. But he didn't have a good time. He was petrified the entire day. That's why we were so surprised that evening when Larry said, "When are we going rafting again? I've never had so much fun in my life!"

Figuring his sudden courage was only because we were safely on our way home, I nonetheless inquired, "How can you go from being so dead set against rafting to suddenly wanting to go again tomorrow, Larry?"

Then he told us that the last time he was in a boat, his friend had drowned. We learned that Larry was convinced that if he ever got into a boat again, somebody in the boat would drown simply because he was there.

Many of the teenagers we encounter have had more trauma by the time they're sixteen than we may know in our entire lifetime. Seeing a friend shot while standing next to him isn't uncommon for many young people today. To effectively minister to them, we must understand some of what they've experienced and how those experiences have contributed to who they are.

How Do Young People Deal With Pain?

Teenagers are hurting. How are they coping with it? Many try to medicate pain through drugs. While teenagers use many different drugs, marijuana is the most popular. Why? As one boy explains, "It's Novocain for the soul."

I've heard many young people state, "I can give up crime. I can give up alcohol. I can even give up sex. But I can't give up *herb*."

Others self-destruct in other ways. Like many teenagers who find themselves in jail, Mike had grown up in an abusive home. Not surprisingly, he began practicing the very thing he hated most.

Mike started sexually abusing his sister at a young age, and he hated himself for it. Even though the abuse had stopped, he couldn't forgive himself. By the time he had completed his sentence and come to live with us, the patterns of failure had been deeply set.

He would sometimes say, "I'd feel more comfortable if you would beat me rather than love me" and "Someday I'm going to commit a crime so bad that I'll go to prison for a long time. Then I can pay for all the wrong things I've done."

Mike did just that. He ran away from our house after only two weeks. Within a few months, he had committed a crime so bad that he was sentenced to ten years in adult prison.

What Mike needed was to remain in a safe, caring environment where he was loved and belonged so he could work through some of his pain. This is what damaged, hurting teenagers need most. Unfortunately, for some, like Mike, this kind of environment comes too late.

Rootless Teenagers

Experts once described youth in trouble as being alienated from society. This alienation was defined as "withdrawing or separation of a person's affections from an object or position of former attachment such as society and family."

But many teenagers like Mike are beyond alienation. Because they never have had an attachment to society or family, they have nothing to be reunited to. They are better defined by the term "anomie": "social instability resulting from a breakdown or absence of standards and values or a sense of dislocation."

Nicky Cruz, the much-feared New York City gang member in the 1950s, knew the same feelings. He tells how he "died" when he was twelve years old. That was the day his mother told him he was the "son of the devil" and she never wanted to see him again. Her statement was the culmination of years of abuse and neglect. Nicky angrily moved out of his home in Puerto Rico and wound up on the streets of New York City. He tells how from that moment on, his body was just waiting to catch up with his dead soul. He no longer cared about anything or anyone. He didn't care if he lived or died.[1] That's what made him so dangerous.

Because of this anomic condition, the concept of rehabilitation has become somewhat outdated as well. "Rehabilitation" means "to restore to a former state." But what does a rootless young person have to be rehabilitated to? This life needs to be re-formed. And that generally happens only in the context of a long-term relationship with a committed, caring adult who makes a place for him or her to belong.

This is precisely what the Apostle Paul did when he made a place in his heart for a frightened, damaged young man, calling him "his very heart." Onesimus belonged. Suddenly he had roots.

WHERE DO ROOTS ORIGINATE?

A healthy sense of belonging usually comes from a healthy family structure. In a more agrarian society, kids were a necessity if the family were to prosper. Everyone had a place, and each one's participation was crucial. Kids were needed to care for younger siblings, cook and clean, work on the farm, tend to elderly grandparents, and perform household chores. They were an asset to the family unit. They were valued.

Things certainly have changed. Many kids aren't viewed as assets today. In some cases they're seen as liabilities. Our western civilization just doesn't need any more kids. We don't need any more doctors or lawyers, let alone unemployed welfare recipients.

Ron Hutchcraft coined the term "paper plate generation." [2] It aptly describes how many young people feel today—unwanted, unneeded, unloved. One girl I met at a Christian camp illustrated such feelings well: "I think about suicide a lot. But my biggest fear is that if I did it, no one would miss me after I was gone."

Yet God doesn't make paper plates. God makes only the finest china and says, "Children are a gift from God...happy is the man who has his quiver full of them" (Psalm 127:3,5 The Living Bible). How can we help kids feel as if they have value—as if they really do belong? We'll examine four very important ways.

CELEBRATING KIDS

One of the most important things we can learn is how to celebrate the lives of kids. Celebrations and parties have become a lost art for many Christians. We have largely given that area over to the devil. When we think of parties, it's often in the bad sense.

We try to celebrate a lot at our house. We have a party every time somebody gets a good report card, gets a driver's license (though inside we're usually agonizing over this one), gets some positive recognition from school—you name it, we find a way to celebrate it. Much of this comes from Hanne's growing up, where celebrations were a central theme of life.

I recall many Valentine's Day mornings sitting at the table with a house full of boys eating heart-shaped pancakes Hanne had created. I must say, sometimes it felt a little strange. But then later, we'd hear one of the guys talking excitedly on the phone about the special breakfast we'd had.

The biggest celebrations always happen on birthdays. The day begins with everybody gathering around the birthday boy's bed, singing "Happy Birthday" and delivering presents. Then we all go downstairs to eat breakfast together. With ten to thirteen of us living at the house, we average one birthday a month.

When Jesse's eighteenth birthday came, we entered his room in the usual way. As we began to sing, his response was very unusual. He pulled the covers over his head. Then he began to shake. We could tell he was sobbing. We left his presents on the floor and went downstairs. When he came down later, he apologized, telling us that this was the first birthday party he had ever had.

As Jesse's birthday approached the next year, he started planning months in advance. He got permission to use the swimming pool of someone in our church, sent out invitations to everyone he could think of, and threw an enormous party.

The Bible is filled with feasts, festivals, and celebrations. God's big on that. God loves for us to celebrate him and all we've been given. This helps remind us who we are, and whose we are.

MAKING YOUTH FEEL NEEDED

Each year teenagers from our home go with us to work at a large Christian conference in Boston. More than eight thousand Christians attend the three-day event, and a great deal of work is required to ensure its success.

Normally, this isn't the kind of event where you'd send a group of troubled teens. Long hours, hard work, and sometimes less than gracious attendees can be a recipe for disaster. But it never has been a disaster.

Though it's not the kind of conference to interest our youth, it always turns out to be one of the highlights of their year. Why? They get dressed up in shirts and ties, wear name badges that say "Conference Staff," attend meetings where they're told how important they are to the success of the event, are given a daily expense allowance for food, and are entrusted with real responsibilities. Every year they're asked to come back and work again because they do such a good job. They feel—and are—needed. And they live up to expectations and beyond.

The best way to get troubled teenagers to the events you want them to attend is to give them responsibility at that event. Have them work in the sound department, set up, greet people, and take the offering. Match them with jobs—important jobs—that they can succeed in and that are consistent with their gifts. You'll find that they'll get more out of it by far than if they were merely sitting in chairs receiving.

CREATING KOINONEA

"Koinonea" is the Greek word for "fellowship." Its interesting definition is "to give, contribute, share; to be initiated into the mysteries of Christ; to participate in the deeds of others, being equally responsible for them."[3]

Embodied in this term "koinonea" is the basic definition of a gang, or at least what many teenagers think a gang is supposed to be. In reality, gangs are only a grossly distorted counterfeit of the real thing. Yet it's unfortunate that gangs often provide more of a sense of commitment, sacrifice, and even the giving of one's life for another, than most churches.

The early church, however, was different. Acts 2:42 says, "They devoted themselves to the apostles' *teaching* and to the *fellowship,* to the *breaking of bread* and to *prayer*" (author's emphasis). Many of us think of church as only a place for teaching and prayer, and thus neglect the aspects of eating together and fellowship. Koinonea fellowship was an essential component of the early church, and it remains necessary for the discipling of young Christians today.

In many cases, the fellowship in prisons and detention center churches can seem more authentic than in most local churches. Perhaps this is because of the stresses and pressures under which inmates live. They need the fellowship of strong Christians to survive. Likewise, the lack of authentic fellowship in our local churches makes it difficult for many released offenders to adjust to church "on the outside."

Involvement in a local church is essential for Christian growth. I have yet to meet a person who has really matured spiritually who wasn't connected to a local church. The church is God's agent for building up God's people. We all must strive to make our own churches havens of real fellowship. This kind of church then becomes the breeding ground for true accountability, the fourth essential element for teenagers' growth and maturity.

PROVIDING ACCOUNTABILITY

In our home, we developed a "Covenant of Commitment." A group of guys who lived with us helped design the original accountability tool. We each sign it, giving others permission to speak the truth into our lives as well as committing to do the same for one another.

Not everyone in our home has been ready for this or wanted it. But for those who have, it has produced more spiritual maturity than perhaps any other thing we do. Nearly every major issue that has surfaced in the lives of teenagers and been resolved has been because of our commitment to mutual accountability.

Damion, one of our first boys, made a statement early on: "I don't think

God is going to move any of us to a deeper level spiritually until we're all together." We have found that this covenant brings us together. See page 93 for a copy of our covenant.

Summary

In this chapter we've been discussing the effects of pain and hurt in the lives of today's young people, and their overwhelming need to belong.

Healthy belonging...

IS NOT

• **an end in itself**—Having a place where teenagers feel they belong is very important. Having a safe place where they can find healing for their pain is essential. Yet if we aren't careful, teenagers can get so focused on their own needs that they come to see Christ as merely a way to solve their problems, rather than the one worthy of surrendering their whole lives to. They need to learn that God isn't a "means to an end"; God is "the end."

IS NOT

• **exclusionary**—We must also be careful that our groups don't exclude others who need to belong. It's easy to become inwardly focused around the needs of our own teenagers, but there's no surer deathblow to the vitality of a youth group. Our teens need to be ever mindful of others around them who are hurting and seek ways to minister to them. And amazingly, this is often how they begin to experience healing themselves. As Jesus said, "Whoever wants to save his life will lose it, but whoever loses his life for me will find it" (Matthew 16:25).

IS NOT

• **merely to meet our needs**—We as leaders also have a strong need to belong. But that never should be met exclusively by the teenagers with whom we minister. I've met youth workers who spend all their leisure time with young people. Teenagers aren't our peers. That's not healthy for adults or young people. We need to have fellowship with people other than our teenagers.

Healthy belonging...

IS

• **something that doesn't happen naturally**—Some youth programs are welcoming environments. Some aren't. The ones that are work hard to make it that way and even harder to keep it that way. Most troubled teenagers won't seek out a youth group. They're usually too insecure to take such initiative.

But even if another teenager or leader happens to get them there once, their insecurity often will lead them to conclude, "Nobody here likes me." Or "The people here all have perfect little lives; they could never understand where I'm coming from." Or "It's clear I don't belong here; they all just want to be with each other." If this young person is ever to return, it will be only because somebody worked really hard to make him or her feel wanted.

IS · more than just feeling comfortable—Creating an environment where teenagers feel comfortable is critically important. Blaring music, friendly youth and leaders, and a teen-friendly meeting environment are all important ways to make teenagers feel comfortable.

But belonging goes above and beyond that. It implies that there's a place where each young person is not only wanted but also needed. Young people may occasionally attend events where they feel comfortable, but they won't want to miss something where they feel needed and important. Work hard to create a place where every teenager you're ministering to can minister.

IS · usually resisted at first—No one likes to feel as if he or she doesn't belong. Yet many troubled teenagers are even more frightened of feeling as if they do belong. For them, it's a potential setup for even more hurt. "Just when I start to trust them, I know they'll turn on me," they reason. Creating an environment of genuine belonging is a long-term commitment, one that will not be without its ups and downs.

ENDNOTES

1. Taken from the video *Jesus Is the Answer* (Go-Tell Communications, 1983).

2. Presented by Ron Hutchcraft in a seminar titled "Sixteen and Lost" at The Billy Graham School of Evangelism in Albany, New York, April 25, 1990.

3. Walter Bauer, *A Greek-English Lexicon of the New Testament and Other Early Christian Literature,* 2nd Ed., revised by William F. Arndt and F. Wilbur Gingrich (Chicago: University of Chicago Press, 1979), 438.

STRAIGHT AHEAD MINISTRIES

Covenant of Commitment

1. I'm asking you to love me enough to tell me the truth about myself as you see it.

> *"Wounds from a friend can be trusted, but an enemy multiplies kisses" (Proverbs 27:6).*

2. I love you enough to commit to confronting you about things I'm concerned about in your life.

> *"Better is open rebuke than hidden love" (Proverbs 27:5).*

3. I give you permission to ask me questions about anything you're concerned about in my life.

> *"Let a righteous man strike me—it is a kindness; let him rebuke me—it is oil on my head. [I] will not refuse it" (Psalm 141:5).*

4. I trust you, that the things you tell me will be in my best interest and out of love for me.

> *"As iron sharpens iron, so one man sharpens another" (Proverbs 27:17).*

Signed:

_____   _____
_____   _____
_____   _____
_____   _____

ACCOUNTABILITY QUESTIONS

1. How have you been doing recently in areas of temptation like drugs, alcohol, sex, foul language, and smoking?
2. How has your attitude been this week toward family, work, friends, and self?
3. Is there somebody you need to forgive or ask to forgive you?
4. How has your time with God been this week? What has been your experience with prayer, reading your Bible, and spending time alone?
5. What kinds of negative things have you allowed into your mind this week? (Think about the impact of music, movies, TV, magazines, and peers.)
6. Is there any area in which you think God is asking you to take another step?

Providing a Place to Belong

Rate your youth ministry in each of the following areas by circling the appropriate number.

1   2   3   4   5

Our youth would prefer to keep the group as it is, without too many new people.

Our group "feels" like a welcoming place; our teenagers work hard to welcome newcomers to the group.

1   2   3   4   5

In our programs, only adults plan, lead, and play significant roles in programs and events.

Our teenagers play critical roles in planning and orchestrating programs and events.

1   2   3   4   5

Our group tends not to be vulnerable about their struggles.

We have regular times of sharing where deep needs and hurts are shared and people are cared for.

1   2   3   4   5

Celebrations haven't been a high priority for our group.

We try to regularly celebrate the lives of our teenagers in specific ways so they know how important they are.

1   2   3   4   5

When teenagers fail, they're often criticized by other teenagers or leaders.

Teenagers can fail and still know they'll be accepted here.

Total score: _____ (Enter this score in the scoring key on page 132.)

CHAPTER 7:
A Dream

Because I lack hope and a sense of purpose in my life, I tend to not plan for tomorrow. Therefore I need a dream or vision for my life so I can make decisions with a long-term perspective.

I would have liked to keep him with me so that he could take your place in helping me while I am in chains for the gospel (Philemon 13).

everal years ago, the pop-recording artist formerly known as Prince wrote "1999," a song about the world ending in the year 2000. The chorus says, "Tonight I'm gonna party like it's 1999." His philosophy of living only for the present continues among teenagers today. We ask, "Why do you throw your lives away?" But they ask, "Why not? If the future holds no hope or sense of purpose for me, why should I bother trying to do good or make long-term plans?"

Every young person needs to know there is a specific purpose for his or her life, a reason to get up in the morning. Without it, life becomes meaningless, as was poignantly illustrated by one teenager's suicide note I saw published in a local newspaper. It simply said, "Not having a good enough reason to live is a good enough reason to die."

We can assure young people that God, the one who created them, has a specific plan and purpose for their lives. As Jeremiah 29:11 says, God has "plans to prosper [them] and not to harm [them]; plans to give [them] hope and a future." Unfortunately, this concept is altogether foreign to many of today's young people.

An Epidemic of Hopelessness

I once asked some teenagers in a detention center if they had any hopes or dreams for the future. One boy responded, "No. That's why we're here."

But it's not only troubled teens who lack a sense of purpose and hope for the future. In one survey, high school students were asked what they felt was the biggest problem with their generation. Their fourth-place answer was "communicating with parents." In third place, they said "drugs and alcohol." But the first two were tied: "loneliness" and "not having anything important to do." [1] Never before have teenagers been busier or exposed to more opportunities, yet felt as lonely and purposeless as they do today.

"SHOW ME A BETTER WAY"

Growing up in a consumer-driven culture, many young people expect more out of life than did previous generations. They aren't satisfied with the same things their parents were. And that's not altogether bad.

I was once leading a Sunday evening service at a church in Maine on the topic of parents and teenagers understanding each other better. To make it more interesting, I asked four teenagers and four parents to sit up front and serve as panelists. I asked each adult to write one question to ask teenagers and each teenager to write one for parents.

Both the questions and the responses were enlightening, especially the final question, which was directed to the young people: "What is your greatest fear?" After several seconds of silence, a high school freshman girl sheepishly raised her hand.

"I think my biggest fear is that I'll work my butt off all through high school to get the best grades so I can get into the best college. Then that I'll work my butt off all through college just so I can get the best job. And then that I'll work my butt off all through my job so I can make the most money, only to be as miserable as my parents are."

We were all stunned by her response. Here was this girl seemingly having a midlife crisis in the ninth grade. But what a good time to have one! At a young age she had already seen through much of the facade of contemporary culture and was longing for something far greater than she had observed, even in the Christian community.

Helping Youth Gain a Sense of Purpose

The Apostle Paul gave a priceless gift to Onesimus. While many may have viewed him as a useless runaway slave, Paul saw something much greater in him. Onesimus had become so useful to Paul that Paul wanted him to become his partner in spreading the gospel. What a boost that must have been for young Onesimus. If an apostle could see that purpose for Onesimus' life, perhaps Onesimus could visualize it too.

Today's young people are exposed to so much information about the world and its problems that they can become overwhelmed, wondering, "What could I possibly do to make a difference?" It is our job to help them discover God's answer to that question in a personal way. Once they do, the course of their lives will be altered forever. Let's look at three things we can do to begin to make that happen.

IMPARTING DREAMS AND VISION

Proverbs 29:18a says, "Where there is no vision, the people perish" (King James Version). I was very insecure as a teenager. In fact, by the eighth grade I had already developed an ulcer, apparently caused by excessive worry, anxiety, and a major inferiority complex. I just didn't feel as if I fit in. But in ninth grade, I heard a missionary speak about smuggling Bibles into Russia. Something clicked inside me. "Wow! I wonder if I could ever do something like that?"

Though I had my share of struggles throughout high school, I never forgot that missionary's message and the possibility that God might use me similarly some day. I believe God planted a vision in my heart way back in ninth grade and it became an anchor for me during my tumultuous teenage years. Ten years after I heard that message, I made the first of many trips smuggling Bibles into China.

It's an incredible thrill to see young people begin to grasp a vision for their lives. As in my case, it becomes a stabilizing force for them. How can we impart such vision? One way is to expose our youth to others with a fiery vision, like the missionary I encountered. But perhaps an even better way is to provide opportunities for them to serve. Then they can experience directly how God can work through them.

For this reason, service projects and mission trips are an essential component of life in the homes we operate. Our teenagers have been to Mexico, Haiti, Ukraine, Ireland, the Dominican Republic, and all over the United States. Before this, most of them had scarcely traveled more than twenty miles from their homes. These trips open their eyes to another whole world. But that's not all they do.

MICHAEL

When we asked Michael, who had lived with us for nearly a year, which of the mission trips he might be interested in, none seemed to capture his interest.

"I don't know," he sighed. "I guess I've always kind of wanted to work with disabled people. Is there anything I can do like that?" We contacted a friend who ran a one-week summer camp for disabled adults. She needed full-time personal care attendants for each attendee, and she met with Michael.

That turned out to be the best week of Michael's life. He called home every day to tell about his adventures with John, the autistic man he was assigned to. His stories were wonderful. When Michael returned home, he said, "You know, this is the first time I've felt like there was a purpose for my life. I think I've finally found what I was made for."

TAMMI

This type of discovery is also important for those raised in the church. There comes a time when teenagers don't need another youth group meeting. They need something far more radical.

Tammi attended the youth ministry we directed while I was in seminary. I couldn't understand why she kept coming, for it was obvious she didn't want to be there. She was one of those teenagers who always sat in the back, giving you a look that says, "I dare you to try to make me have a good time." If any event had the potential of being a hit, hopes were dashed the moment Tammi showed up. She had the gift of discouragement. Her attitude could squelch any party.

We had just started taking our suburban youth to Boston weekly to feed the homeless. The first two weeks went great. Then on the third week Tammi showed up. "Here we go again. Another great evening down the drain," I thought.

As we started to sing in the van, Tammi just rolled her eyes and stared out the window. When we pulled up to the first stop, everyone got out to distribute coffee, soup, sandwiches, and blankets. Nearby I overheard one of the homeless men asking Tammi where we were from. "We're a Christian youth group from Framingham," she said.

"Well, I hate God," he quickly countered.

When asked why, he replied, "Cause God killed my wife." Hearing the anger in his voice, I wondered if I should go over and rescue her. But I decided, "No. I'd rather see *her* squirm for a change."

Tammi responded, "You know, I'd probably feel the same way if I were you."

"Huh, that's not a bad answer," I thought.

When we rounded up the teenagers to go to the next site, I noticed seven homeless people huddled together. As I walked over, I realized that Tammi was standing in the middle. And the man who had spoken of his hatred toward God was addressing the group. "You know, you guys really need to get your lives back on track with God. And you need to start going to church, too."

"What's been going on here?" I wondered.

When I motioned for Tammi to go to the van, it was obvious that she wasn't interested in leaving her new friends. We waited a little longer, and then I had to literally put my arm around her and pull her toward to the van. She continued her conversation with them all the while, until finally she was on board. Gathered outside her window was the small band of men, smiling from ear to ear and waving goodbye.

As we drove away, Tammi held her hand over her eyes; she was crying. She was very quiet the rest of the night. But there was a marked difference in her after that. Tammi didn't need another youth group meeting; she needed to have her heart opened. And that's what happened that Monday evening.

Part of the reason Tammi had been miserable was because she had no sense of purpose in her life. But now she had experienced firsthand that she could make a difference in someone's life. As a result, she decided to go to a Christian college and major in social work.

DISCOVERING SPIRITUAL GIFTS

Scripture clearly teaches that the Holy Spirit has given each Christian spiritual gifts, which are listed in Romans 12:6-8; 1 Corinthians 12:8-10, 28; and Ephesians 4:11. But most teenagers are too insecure and self-conscious to recognize their gifts. In fact, most probably would argue that they were somehow "passed over" when gifts were being handed out.

Therefore, it's our responsibility to help them discover their spiritual gifts, to educate them in how to use them, and to provide them with opportunities to exercise them. There are a myriad of spiritual gift inventories available that can be administered to help teenagers identify particular gifts. Most take no more than thirty minutes to complete. Don and Katie Fortune have even developed one specifically designed for youth. It's in their book *Discover Your Children's Gifts.*[2] The book also lists 180 different careers and job possibilities that are well suited for people with various gifts.

But even if you don't have the opportunity to administer a spiritual gifts inventory, begin to notice what your young people are good at. It will become obvious whether they have gifts of mercy, hospitality, administration, leadership, giving, teaching, discernment, or one of the others. Note also the types of people they tend to be drawn to. Are they naturally gifted with children, elderly, those who are hurting, or their peers?

What you may observe quickly, they are probably oblivious to. That's why we must point out their gifts clearly, stressing that these are gifts of the Holy Spirit. They don't have them because they somehow deserve them but because God chose to give them to them. And now they have a responsibility to use them for God's glory, as Jesus taught in the parable of the talents (Matthew 25:14-30).

BLESSING ONE ANOTHER

With a group of young people who know each other, try this powerful exercise. Hand out a list of the spiritual gifts, briefly explaining each. Then have the entire group focus for five minutes or so on each person. For each teenager, ask the group, "What spiritual gift(s) do you think this person has, and why do you think so?" Then ask, "What types of people do you see this person being most effective with, and why?"

While some may feel a little embarrassed at first by all the attention focused on them, they'll never forget the things said about them. This is a tangible exercise in "blessing" one another.

Just a word of caution: As you go from person to person, be sure there is never a long period of silence before something is spoken about someone, or that will be what the person remembers. The young person will see that hesitation as evidence that he or she doesn't have any gifts. In some cases you may need to prime the pump by speaking up first, especially for those teenagers others may not know as well.

Once you've helped your students identify their gifts, seek to provide tangible opportunities for them to serve in their unique areas of giftedness. Every youth ministry should strive to have each young person participate in ongoing service projects and/or summer mission trips. These activities should be tailored to the heart, gifting, and calling of each person so all of them can experience God using them in their own areas of giftedness.

OPPORTUNITIES TO SACRIFICE

Teenagers generally live up to our expectations. Tony explained to us that his father would say, "I'll visit you in prison, but I'll never visit you in a hospital." In other words, *Get them before they get you!* No small wonder Tony was in prison for assaulting another teenager. Kids often give us exactly what we expect. When we expect too little, we do them a grave disservice.

Young people want to strive for great things, and they aren't afraid to sacrifice to achieve them. When I asked Kevin (the boy mentioned in chapter 1) why he had joined a gang, he said, "At first it was for protection. Being in a new neighborhood, it was hard to get by without it. But more than that, it was something I felt I could be proud to be a part of. It also gave my life a moral structure. The gang required honor, integrity, and loyalty. And for the first time in my life, I had a goal, something to strive for. I wanted to climb up to a position in the gang where I would be recognized and given respect by everyone. And I would do whatever it took to get that."

If we don't present teenagers with a big enough challenge, someone else will. One of the fastest growing sects in American prisons is "The Five Percenters," a radical, militant offshoot from the Nation of Islam. What makes them so popular? For one thing, they demand very high levels of sacrifice and commitment from their members. People respect that and are willing to join.

Jesus could never be accused of making it too easy for people to follow him. On one occasion many of his disciples turned back and no longer followed him, saying his teachings were too hard (John 6:60-66).

He presented this challenge in Matthew 10:39: "Whoever loses his life for my sake will find it." Many of us have personally experienced the reality of that verse. We first became involved in youth work as a sacrifice to God, but in the process discovered that we were the ones who were being truly blessed. We must give our teenagers that same opportunity to sacrifice their lives in service to God and others.

FINDING LIFE

Sometimes I look back at the photos of the first group of suburban teenagers we took to Haiti. We spent the first weekend at a conference center in New Hampshire preparing for the trip. In those photos, our hair was neatly arranged, and our clothes were spotless. We looked good, but our eyes revealed that most were insecure and self-absorbed.

What a difference between those photos and the ones shot ten days later. After days without showers, clean clothes, mirrors to apply makeup, hair dryers, or curling irons, our appearances weren't nearly as attractive. But our eyes looked altogether different. They sparkled. They were filled with joy.

It has been said that the eyes are the windows to the soul. And significant things were taking place in the depths of our souls. Like the day we visited Mother Teresa's Home for Abandoned Children. When we entered that building, the sounds of crying children filled the air. But as we walked from room to room, picking up children along the way, the crying began to still. Rather than putting children back in their cribs when we exited a room as directed, our young people added more to their arms in each room we entered. It made the nuns a little nervous, but the sounds of laughter and joy more than compensated for the confusion.

I had the distinct feeling that this may have been the first time some of our students had ever felt so wanted, needed, and important. It was a small thing we were doing, but what joy their presence brought into that place. It was hard to leave. Prying clinging children and crying babies from our teenagers was torturous.

We had seen so much poverty and devastation in Haiti, yet at the same time we had experienced so much joy. Every evening our discussions were lively. "How could God allow these people to live in such horrible circumstances, while we live in such luxury?" "Why did so many of them seem so much happier than we are?"

In the following months, I received college reference forms from some of those youths. Several contained notes like "I still want to be a nurse, but now I would like to go back to Haiti and work with those children after I graduate. I just keep thinking about them." or "I'm considering changing my major to teaching. It seems like there's such a need for that over in Haiti." These teenagers had thought they were sacrificing when they decided to spend a couple weeks in Haiti; instead they began to find life.

Summary

We've discussed the epidemic of hopelessness that runs rampant among our youth and the need to impart dreams into their lives by helping them actualize their gifts.

A spiritual gift...

IS NOT • **merely for our own fulfillment**—God's gifts and calling are to build up others, not just to bring us fulfillment and joy. The moment we become selfish in our motivation, the joy is quickly gone. It's only when we have the proper attitude of serving God and others that joy begins to flood our own souls. But that's always a byproduct.

IS NOT • **to be misspent**—Romans 11:29 states that God's gifts and call are irrevocable. That means our gifts can be used for good or evil. Many people have used their God-given gifts of leadership to lead people down destructive paths. We must continually reinforce to our young people the responsibility they have to use their gifts for good.

IS NOT • **a cause for boasting**—Each of us has unique gifts and callings from

God. We don't have them because we deserve them. We have them because God gave them to us. Therefore, we can't boast of how great we are, but only of the goodness of God.

A spiritual gift...

IS • **more often caught than taught**—Most teenagers haven't had enough life experience to know what they're really good at. They need opportunities to try new and different things. It's in that process that they discover what things really gel with them. And sometimes what gels for them is not what they might have expected. That's why it's so important to give them as many varied kinds of experiences as possible.

IS • **what gives focus and direction**—We operate best and glorify God most, when we operate within our areas of giftedness. Knowing our gifts also helps us gain a greater sense of our mission and calling. When we know what God has called us to, we can more easily discern what things we should say yes to and what we should say no to. The Apostle Paul had that kind of clear focus, as evidenced in the fact that he opened nearly all his letters with the words "Paul, called to be an apostle of Jesus Christ, by the will of God." He wouldn't allow himself to be sidetracked from that mission, and the world was changed because of it.

ENDNOTES

1. Survey conducted and cited by Guy Doud in a general session at Youth Specialties National Youth Workers Convention in Chicago, 1988.

2. Don and Katie Fortune, *Discover Your Children's Gifts* (Grand Rapids, MI: Chosen Books, 1993).

Imparting Vision and Dreams Into Young People

Rate your youth ministry in each of the following areas by circling the appropriate number.

1   **2**   **3**   **4**   **5**

We don't have mission trips or service projects available for our teenagers at this time.

Every student in our program is given the opportunity to participate in mission trips and service projects.

1   **2**   **3**   **4**   **5**

Most of our teenagers probably don't know their spiritual gifts.

We have our teenagers take spiritual gifts inventories, and we help them understand and apply them.

1   **2**   **3**   **4**   **5**

We try not to place high expectations on our teenagers.

We believe and expect great things from our youth.

1   **2**   **3**   **4**   **5**

We tend to place our adult leaders where we have the greatest needs.

We know what gifts our adult leaders have, and we work to make sure they're functioning in them.

1   **2**   **3**   **4**   **5**

Our adult leaders bear all the responsibility in our program.

We try to find something important for each of our young people to do.

Total score: _____ (Enter this score in the scoring key on page 132.)

CHAPTER 8:
Empowerment and Healthy Boundaries

Because I feel powerless, without many positive options, I tend to rebel in unhealthy ways. Therefore I need empowerment and healthy boundaries so I can move toward healthy independence.

Perhaps the reason he was separated from you for a little while was that you might have him back for good—no longer as a slave, but better than a slave, as a dear brother (Philemon 15-16a).

Onesimus. Would you risk your own good reputation on a guy like him? Paul did. And he asked Philemon to do the same. In first-century Rome, Onesimus didn't have many options. At best, he might spend much of his remaining life in prison. At worst, he could be put to death.

Rather than viewing Onesimus in his current state, Paul knew God had a plan for him. So he asked Philemon to free Onesimus, to make him an equal, something virtually unheard of in that day. To Paul, this was far more important than any economic advantage or justice that might be due Philemon.

Yet for this slave, Onesimus, to successfully transition into the free world, he would need more than just his "freedom" documents. A slave can become free in a moment's time, but it can take a lifetime for a person to heal from the effects of a slavery mentality. It's the same for troubled teens. And while their needs are legion, sometimes the "help" we offer them can be more detrimental than helpful.

What Is *Really* Helpful?

Marcus had lived with us for more than two years and was transitioning into living on his own. Because of his low income and the fact that he was still in school, he qualified to receive health insurance through Medicare.

I took Marcus to the welfare building, but as soon as we entered the agent's office, he assumed an entirely different demeanor. I was embarrassed by the negative, sarcastic attitude he was displaying. As we got in the car Marcus said angrily, "Who does he think he is, trying to tell me what I'm supposed to do?"

More than a little perturbed, I countered, "Wait a minute. Who do you think you are, coming off with an attitude like that? He was trying to help you, and all you could do was insult him. What's up with that?"

"I don't need his kind of help," was his response.

Later, as I reflected upon the situation, I realized the agent wasn't the issue at all. At issue was everything he and the system represented to Marcus. It all made him feel inferior, incompetent, and inadequate.

Sometimes when we try to help troubled teenagers, our efforts conjure up for them feelings of inferiority. In their mind, we place them in a subservient position. For this reason, we've changed the name of our mentoring program to a leadership development program. It's an attempt to remove the imagery so often associated with mentoring—where the stronger helps the weaker.

The same situation arises when people ask to be "pen pals" with incarcerated teens. It usually doesn't work. The prospect of having another person try to help them just isn't very appealing to teenagers. They already feel inadequate enough.

I remember one incident when we brought some friends with us into a juvenile jail. One of the women got to meet Daryle. She had heard us talk about how much God was using him in that facility. As we were leaving, she asked Daryle if he would write to her son, who was much younger and needed some wise counsel from an older brother-type person.

Daryle's face lit up. This mother was saying her son needed him. Daryle took that very seriously. He wrote letters to that younger boy, investing tremendous amounts of time explaining some of the things he had learned from the Lord.

Young people like Daryle thrive when we empower them with our trust. Yet sadly, not all teenagers are at that place. It's a very important distinction to be made: "Does this individual really want what we have to offer?"

"DO YOU WANT TO GET WELL?"

Jesus had an interesting encounter with a thirty-eight year-old man who had been paralyzed from birth. John 5:6 records, "When Jesus saw him lying there and learned that he had been in this condition for a long time, he asked him, 'Do you want to get well?' "

That seems like a foolish question to ask someone who spends every day hanging out at a "healing pool." Of course he wants to get well. But listen to this man's response: "Sir, I have no one to help me into the pool when the water is stirred. While I am trying to get in, someone else goes down ahead of me."

Jesus was asking for a simple yes or no answer. Instead he heard an excuse. Perhaps the question didn't have such an obvious answer after all. "Getting well" can be intimidating and frightening. Getting well has its own set of consequences.

If this man were to get well, he probably would be expected to get a job—for the first time. He would be expected to find a place to live and start being responsible for many new things. He would be expected to begin living a completely different life than he was used to. Getting well would mean making new friends. Until now, he had only hung out at this familiar pool. The people he knew were the blind, the lame, and the paralyzed (John 5:3). Would he even be able to make it in this other world? I've learned not to underestimate the importance of Jesus' question.

DENNIS

Dennis had lived with us for three months when he came home one night completely drunk. Rather than dealing with him in that state, we decided to wait until morning. When Hanne and I spoke to him, his response was, "You just don't understand. I've been an alcoholic since I was twelve years old. My mother's an alcoholic. My father's an alcoholic. My grandparents are alcoholics. It's all I'll ever be."

"But Dennis," we said, "You're a new person now. God has made you new. The old you is gone."

"No. I've tried changing before. I knew it was just a matter of time before I'd fall right back into the same old stuff. I'm surprised I lasted this long."

"But we want to help you Dennis. We'll talk with you every day about it. We'll hold you accountable."

"You don't know me," he argued. "This is just who I am."

Finally it dawned on us. We were convinced that Dennis could change. We were willing to do whatever it took. But was he?

Then Hanne asked him, "Dennis do you want to get well?"

"I already told you. I'm an alcoholic. My mother's an alcoholic..."

"But Dennis, do you want to get well? Do you want to change?" Hanne interrupted.

There was a long silence. "No. No, I guess not," he finally sighed.

It's an important question. Someone once said, "Until the pain of staying the same becomes greater than the pain of changing, nobody will ever choose change." Jesus invested most heavily in those who already had felt the pain of staying the same and wanted to change, whatever the cost. He clearly stated, "It is not the healthy who need a doctor, but the sick. I have not come to call the righteous, but sinners" (Mark 2:17).

Shortly after that, Dennis left our home. We couldn't do anymore for him because he didn't want what we had to offer.

Rebellion: The Trademark of Youth?

Teenagers are in a precarious period of their lives. On one hand, they're confident and self-assured; on the other, hopelessly insecure. They're at a stage where they need to be empowered to make their own decisions, yet at times guarded from their own destructive choices. It's during this transition period—enjoying some of the freedom of responsible adults, yet still being sheltered from some of the risks that come with living independently—that what we have come to term "rebellion" most often surfaces.

Thus, to many, the terms "teenager" and "rebellion" seem almost interchangeable. I came across a quote that seems to sum up this age group rather well: "Our youth now love luxury, they have bad manners and contempt for authority...They no longer rise when elders enter the room. They contradict their parents, chatter before company, gobble up their food and tyrannize their teachers." [1]

This may sound like somebody's description of the teens you work with, but it was actually written by Socrates, who died in 399 B.C. Teenage rebellion truly has been around for a long time.

But how do we know how much rebellion to allow in the teenagers we work with? How do we best confront rebellion while still preserving relationships? When do we allow teenagers to suffer the consequences for their actions, and when do we step in to keep them from getting hurt? How do we keep empowering them during this rocky time of transition?

Here are four principles we've learned about dealing with teenagers and rebellion. We've learned most of them the hard way.

TEENAGERS NEED TO REBEL

It took me a long time to figure out that my definition of success and our teenagers' definition of success are very different. To me, success was getting a kid to *do the right thing*. "Don't hang around with that crowd." "Say no to drugs and alcohol." "Do your daily devotions." If by some miracle I could get them to do all the right things, I'd succeeded!

The only problem is this: In the minds of teenagers, even if they do the right things—they don't go to that party, they do their homework, they don't go out with that boy or girl, they stay away from the wrong crowd, they come home on time, and so on—in their minds, *they've failed* if they haven't made those decisions on their own. Teenagers would rather make the wrong decisions but truly make *their* own decisions. Why? Because teenagers tend to define success as *doing their own thing*.

This reality was made clear with Jason. He started getting into trouble with the friends he was hanging out with, so we grounded him. For a couple of weeks he was restricted to our house unless he was at school, at work, or with somebody else from the house. During that period we observed that he was particularly difficult to wake up for school. He was always tired. That didn't make any sense to us, for he was at home now more than ever.

One day, after Jason's grounding was over, he said to us, "You probably noticed how tired I was during the past few weeks."

"Yes, we certainly did notice. Why were you so tired?"

"Well, believe it or not, I would get up at one or two o'clock in the morning, when everyone else was sleeping, and walk around outside."

"Oh, great. What were you doing, hooking up with your old friends?" we asked.

"No. Nobody's out on our street at that time of the night."

"Were you drinking by yourself then?"

"No, I wasn't drinking. I wasn't doing anything. I was just walking."

"Are you still doing it?" we continued probing.

"No. I don't do it anymore."

"When did you stop?"

"When my grounding was over."

"So why did you do it, Jason?"

"I don't know. I guess—just because you said I couldn't."

Somehow in Jason's mind, he was succeeding. He was doing his own thing. The key, then, is to empower teenagers to make the *right* decisions by involving them in the process so they feel like they made the decisions.

We know a Christian couple with three wonderful children who have all completed college and gone on into adulthood with relatively few hitches. We asked them what parenting gems they could impart to us. One of their core philosophies was the recognition that all teenagers have a need to rebel.

"We don't make it our goal to get them *not* to rebel at all. Instead, we try to steer them toward rebelling in those areas that aren't big issues to us. For example, our son Steven has never liked to clean his room. To us it wasn't a big deal either, but we didn't let him know that. In fact, we insisted he keep his room clean. He rarely did. But it was sort of his area to rebel in. We're just grateful it was that and not a host of other possible things."

While this philosophy works well with most teenagers, some teenagers are just more rebellious by nature. For these, the approach of *majoring on the majors* works much better. Don't make every issue into an issue. And when you do have to choose, I recommend not making hairstyle, earrings, clothing, or music the major issues.

TEENAGERS NEED PRACTICE MAKING DECISIONS

The term "adolescence" is defined by Webster as "the state or process of growing up." It's interesting that other mammals with a similar life expectancy as humans attain full adulthood by year two or three. In fact, no animal has nearly as prolonged a maturation period as we human beings. Perhaps it has to do with our being created in the "image of God." We were created with the freedom to choose, as opposed to the raw instinct animals possess. Adolescence, then, is the stage where *freedom of choice* is given the opportunity to develop in a healthy way.

If, in fact, adolescence encompasses the transition time to adulthood, then it stands to reason that most teenagers should be quite independent by the time they're eighteen years old and getting ready to leave home. Ideally, a senior in high school would have few if any rules at all. "Oh no," most parents would respond. "Not in my house! If he's going to live under my roof, he's going to live under my rules!"

I agree—if there are major areas of rebellion involved, such as drug abuse, criminal activity, or other harmful behavior influencing younger siblings. For many types of rebellion, though, the safest place for teenagers to fail and get back on their feet again is while they're still living at home. Teenagers need opportunities to slowly gain independence before they're on their own.

A Lesson From the Amish

The Amish are undoubtedly one of the most conservative groups in American culture. But they have an interesting approach to raising teenagers. For teenagers in their last year at home, all structure and restrictions are lifted. As would be expected, these teenagers typically go crazy for that year. They party, stay out late, and run around with their peers. It must be painful for parents to watch what happens with their sons and daughters during that period.

At the end of the year, the teenagers are confronted with a decision.

"Do you want to stay within the Amish faith and community, or do you want to leave it?" If they choose to stay, they must abide by all the rules and standards expected. About half of them decide to stay. They've tasted what sin and secular society have to offer, and they've concluded that the "forbidden fruit" isn't as good as they may have once thought.

Likewise, the prodigal son didn't want to come home until he had first tasted what sin had to offer and found it wasn't all it was cracked up to be. Though the father continued loving him all the while, he never chased or rescued him from the clutches of sin. He was simply there, once his son "came to his senses."

SHORT-CIRCUITING THE PROCESS

When we try to protect teenagers from the pain we've gone through, we can short-circuit what God is doing in their lives and sometimes inflict more pain on them in the long run. The prodigal son wasn't ready for real change until he had "hit the wall." We all must come to Christ on our own time frame, and often that's not until we hit bottom. We dare not short-circuit that process in the lives of the teenagers with whom we're ministering.

Does that mean we shouldn't issue consequences to teens? Not at all. But perhaps we need to rethink why and how we issue consequences. In each situation we need to ask, "What is it that will help this young person the most in the long run? How can I empower this teenager to make better decisions and to learn from poor decisions already made?"

When I was a resident assistant in a state university dormitory, I always dreaded those first couple of months of the first semester. I spent many mornings cleaning up vomit from partying freshmen who had left home for the first time and couldn't handle the freedom. They were getting drunk every night, skipping classes the next morning, and flunking out by midterms. Sadly, many of the teenagers who partied hardest were from conservative Christian families. They were experiencing their first real taste of freedom.

One Christian couple we know sent their son off to college. Everyone expected him to do well. He had always made good grades in high school, faithfully attended youth group functions, and was by all appearances a good kid. That's why his parents were so shocked when they learned at midterm that he was failing every class.

When he came home on break, he didn't even resemble the clean-cut boy who had left home only a couple of months before. His hair hadn't been cut, he had bags under his eyes, and by the looks of his luggage, he hadn't visited a laundromat since he moved out.

What had happened? Had college ruined him? No. It merely had revealed things about him that had been previously hidden. Upon further reflection, his parents realized that the mother had always made sure he got up for school, insisted he do his homework every night, kept his room clean, and so on. When mom was out of the picture, he quickly fell apart. Fortunately, he learned some difficult lessons that semester and ended up pulling through.

To short-circuit teenagers' need for independence can hurt them in one of two ways: Either they'll become so insecure and incompetent that they'll be afraid to make any decisions on their own, or they'll go against everything their parents stand for.

A good friend of ours grew up with a very controlling, stifling father. And while our friend is a very wise and learned Christian now, he has consistently stayed away from institutions of higher learning. Why? He says it's because his father always told him he needed to go to college if he was ever going to amount to anything. Subconsciously, he's made it his life's ambition to prove his father wrong.

I remember reading one survey of high school-age students that revealed teenagers feel they do what they want to do only 20 percent of the time; 80 percent of the time they don't feel they have a choice in what they're doing. What things can we do to empower teenagers to make more of their own decisions, to more adequately prepare them for life? Part of this includes giving them a voice in the consequences they receive for making bad decisions.

We ask the youth in our house to come up with consequences they feel will teach them the most. Surprisingly, their consequences are often stiffer than ours would have been. And when they come up with them, they're also much more likely to learn from them and to abide by them.

TEENAGERS NEED OUR CONFIDENCE IN THEM

In my senior year of college, I had to choose between two job offers. One was several states away. The other was in my hometown. I had refrained from asking my parents for advice, mostly because I already knew what they would say: "Just take the job back here. Then you can move back home with us for a while until you get on your feet and can afford your own place." I didn't want to hear that.

Yet there I was, the day before I had to make a decision, and I had no idea what to do. Finally at 10:30 that night, I broke down and called my parents to get their opinion. I was shocked when they said, "We really don't know what you should do, Scott. But we do know that you hear from the Lord, and we're confident that you will make the right choice." They caught me completely off guard. Now the pressure was on me. I had to hear from the Lord. And their believing in me empowered me to do just that.

I ended up accepting the job in my hometown. I even moved back home for a while. It was, without a doubt, the right decision. But I also know that had my parents tried to convince me to move back home, I would have chosen the other job.

When we empower young people with our confidence in their decision-making, we give them a wonderful gift. When guys in our home are facing a decision, we often talk with them about some of the options before them, pointing out pros and cons.

Then we say, "We've seen you make good choices in the past," and then we detail past incidents where we've seen successful decisions. "We know you have the ability to hear from God, and we believe you'll hear from God again in this situation. We're not going to make this decision for you. We're entrusting you with it, and we really believe you'll do the right thing."

Do they always make the right decisions? No. But then we can say, "We were really surprised about the choice you made. It didn't seem consistent with where you had been going and what we knew you to be capable of doing. What do you think happened?" Sometimes the process of talking through bad choices they've made contributes more to their learning and maturity than the good choices they've made.

TEENAGERS WANT AND NEED BOUNDARIES

The dictionary defines rebellion as "the act of resisting or opposing the controls." Just as teens have a need to rebel, they also have a need for controls, or boundaries. Obviously, as young people grow older, the boundaries need to widen. But no matter where the boundaries are, teenagers will bounce off them. And once the boundaries are removed, they may "go crazy" for a while. But usually they move back to where the boundaries were previously placed, as illustrated below.

Teenagers need boundaries. They need to test them and to bounce off them if they're going to develop in a healthy way. But when the boundaries aren't clearly set in the home, the next boundaries are usually at school, and teenagers bounce off them. When boundaries aren't enforced at school, the next boundary is often the law, and teenagers bounce off it. But there is no one more miserable than a young person who has no clear sense of boundaries.

Tommy was in a detention center Bible study where we were talking about rules. He commented, "I could do anything I wanted growing up. No one ever told me I had to go to school, when I had to be home at night, or anything. No one ever put any rules on me."

"Oh, here we go," I thought, "He's bragging about not having any rules. If only he understood..."

Then Tommy looked down as he continued, "I guess there just wasn't much love in my home."

The opposite of love isn't always hate. Sometimes it's just not caring.

Boundaries are not only restrictive, they also provide a sense of security for young people. Psalm 16:5-6 says, "Lord, you have assigned me my portion and my cup; you have made my lot secure. The boundary lines have fallen for me in pleasant places; surely I have a delightful inheritance."

MACHETES

Several years ago we led a team of high school students on a mission trip to Haiti. One day several of the boys were bartering with the vendors in a local market. They were very proud to buy machete knives, complete with leather cases to house the thirty-inch blade, for only five dollars each. They obviously hadn't given much thought to getting them through U.S. Customs, but it was a great bargain nonetheless.

Now that they owned these beautiful weapons of destruction, they had a dilemma. There was no place to use them—until someone noticed a few trees outside the window of the church where we were staying. They marveled at how easily those branches could be lopped off.

The next morning, the neighbor stormed over to the church, demanding to see the pastor. He was furious about what had happened to his trees! Little did these boys know that trees are a rare and precious commodity in Haiti and that they had done a great deal of damage not only to this neighbor but to church relations as well.

Needless to say, we had a very difficult meeting that evening with our team. I was very angry. We talked for a long time about what had happened and about what should be done about it. The youth expressed their frustrations as well. I then put it back in their court, asking them to come up with solutions on how to resolve the problem. They decided that the guys involved should pay the man for his damaged trees, which they did. But all in all, it wasn't a fun night.

On the return flight, everyone had to fill out an evaluation form on the trip. On my form, the machete incident definitely stood out as the low point. I expected to see lots of negative comments from the youth about that difficult evening meeting as well. Instead, the opposite happened. That meeting was consistently listed as one of the highlights of the trip! It confirmed to me just how much teenagers like to know where the boundaries are and to see them enforced. It makes them feel secure.

Types of Rebellion

Every teenager exhibits some type of rebellion, with the possible exception of people like my wife, who turned from a reprobate life of sin and shame at age three and hasn't really wavered much since.

Though most teenagers rebel, there are different types of rebellion. They vary according to the individual makeup of the young person as well as the current issues confronting his or her life. Thus, it's important for us to understand the teenagers we're ministering to and where they're coming from before deciding on a strategy to deal with their rebellion. Let's examine several different types of rebellion.

PASSIVE REBELLION

This type of rebellion characterized me as a young person. I was the most agreeable person you would ever encounter. If you asked me to do something, I would seldom say no. But if it were something I didn't want to do, I just wouldn't do it. Likewise, if I wanted to do something, regardless of whether or not I had been given permission, I would do it. I lived by the philosophy "It's easier to get forgiveness than permission."

Rarely did people have conflicts with me. I would seldom argue with anyone. I just quietly did whatever I pleased. And in those rare times when I was caught doing something wrong, I would simply apologize and promise to try harder the next time.

Another form of passive rebellion is that of procrastination. Martin, a boy who lived with us for two years, would always agree to anything we asked him to. It's just that it always had to be on his timetable. Whenever we confronted him, he would never say he wouldn't do it. He just hadn't gotten to it yet. But we could be assured, it was next on his list. Consequently, if his weekly chores got done once a month, he was doing well.

Teenagers who are passive rebels are very frustrating to deal with. Jesus had a hard time with them too. In Matthew 21:28-31 he told a parable of a father who asked his two sons to go into the vineyard and work. The first said, "I will not," but then later changed his mind and went. The second said, "I will, sir," but then didn't go. Jesus' harshest words were reserved for the second. Likewise, in Revelation 3:16, God reserved his strongest words for the church in Laodicea, saying, "Because you are lukewarm—neither hot nor cold—I am about to spit you out of my mouth."

What's the best approach with this kind of teenager? Somehow, these kids must be challenged with the benefits of radical obedience to Christ: If they're faithful in little things, God will entrust them with big things (Matthew 25:21). Exhorting them to "just say no" isn't a big enough incentive. They must see the benefits of saying yes to God in the big things and in the little things, somehow understanding that this is the very gateway through which we can experience God's miraculous intervention.

ACTIVE REBELLION

While passive rebels are difficult to work with, it's the active rebels who cause you to lose your hair, and the strands you manage to save quickly turn gray. A parent's lament of such a child is often, "I've tried everything. I've grounded her, taken away every privilege, removed her favorite items from her room, and even ignored her. Nothing seems to work."

Teenagers actively rebel in different ways and for different reasons. It's important to understand which category a young person may fit into because that will affect the approach you need to take. Let's consider three types of active rebels: strong-willed children, rebels against authority, and circumstantial rebels.

Strong-Willed Children

We knew after two days that Sarah, our firstborn, was a strong-willed child. From the time she got home from the hospital, she knew exactly what she wanted and had the ability to stay with the course long enough to see it through. She's been that way ever since.

To go nose-to-nose with a strong-willed child in a power struggle is only giving them what they want. And in the end, they'll most likely win anyway. You can't outlast or break a strong-willed child—nor do you want to. These young people will ultimately change the world. The question is, will it be for better or for worse? The answer depends upon what obstacles they're tearing down. The last thing we want to do with strong-willed teenagers is to break their spirits. Rather, their energies usually need to be redirected.

I've found that the best thing to do with strong-willed teenagers is to acknowledge their leadership abilities. I tell them how much I need them if I'm going to get through to their friends or maintain control in the youth group. "They'll listen to you more than me," I say. "Can you help me by getting them to be quiet and attentive during our meetings?"

"Sure, no problem," they usually respond. "I'll take care of them."

I also try to give the most responsibilities to these youth, the very ones who are the biggest troublemakers. In most cases, they rise to our level of expectations. These youth can raise havoc against the kingdom of darkness when the Lord channels their energies.

Again, mission trips and service projects are some of the most effective experiences to involve these teenagers in. Giving them opportunities to rebel against the evils of poverty, racism, or injustice positions them to be a force for good to be reckoned with. If we don't steer them to larger and more appropriate battles, they'll tend to fight against all the stuff we want them to embrace.

REBELS AGAINST AUTHORITY

For some teenagers, any authority figure brings out the worst in them. As we discussed in chapter 3, this often is manifested when a child's relationship with his or her first authority figure, usually a father but sometimes a mother, was unhealthy.

Simply applying more structure, authority, and control only serves to exacerbate the problem. Instead, a new and deeper relationship with a parent or parental figure must be developed. Only as this relationship improves can this individual begin to respect other forms of authority.

This young person is living proof of the equation *rules minus relationship equals rebellion.* It's clear why God so strongly warns, "Parents, don't be hard on your children. If you are, they might give up" (Colossians 3:21, Contemporary English Version).

CIRCUMSTANTIAL REBELLION

Circumstantial rebellion is rooted not so much in the personality of the young person as in the struggles going on around the individual at a particular time. As irrational as this young person may appear, there usually is a specific situation causing the behavior.

Try to understand from his or her perspective the pressures the youth may be experiencing. Anxiety, guilt, depression, fear of failure, insecurity, or strained friendships can all contribute to a teenager's state of rebellion.

When it appears that outside influences are negatively influencing a young person, it's important to work primarily on the relationship, keeping your comments and advice brief. Often teenagers can't even verbalize what's stressing them, but if they sense that you're on their side and not against them, you can begin working on it together.

In some cases, however, particularly where destructive behavior is involved, it's important to voice your concerns. I often say, "I'm concerned about you, but I'm not sure what role I should play in this. I really care about you and want to help. What do you think would be most useful for me to do or not to do?" This empowers them to grant me permission to provide input into their lives, a very important role for them. It also keeps our relationship from becoming the object of strain and the focus of conflict.

Summary

Teenagers and rebellion—unfortunately the two often go hand-in-hand. But I was encouraged by the results I read from interviews of people who were serving the Lord ten years after high school. The survey attempted to discover common denominators among these young adults. Amazingly, those factors were (1) they were raised in an environment where they saw authentic faith lived and (2) they rebelled against it for a time.

The next chapter examines what it means for us to live out authentic faith before young people.

Empowerment and healthy boundaries...

ARE NOT • **a way to relinquish our responsibility**—Some youth workers may see empowering others as a way to either unload unpleasant and tedious tasks or to avoid the responsibility for a youth program. Healthy empowering is neither.

In fact, empowering others will actually increase your level of responsibility, even though you may not be doing everything. Empowering others involves training them, knowing them well enough that you can give them appropriate tasks, and then monitoring them to ensure their success.

It's usually easier to do things yourself than to entrust others with the responsibility. But unless we involve others, we rob them of the opportunity to grow and thrive, and we miss the privilege of seeing God work in and through them. Our role should become one of serving our teenagers and other adult leaders so they can be empowered to minister. And sometimes that means we take on the more menial tasks.

ARE NOT • **the same for everybody**—Every teenager has unique gifts, and each has a different level of maturity and leadership ability. What is empowering for one person may be drudgery and a setup for failure for another. We must prayerfully get to know our students and leaders, asking God for wisdom on how to best empower them in Kingdom work.

ARE NOT • **exclusively ours to decide**—Most of the teenagers we work with have at least one parent, and those parents are ultimately responsible for their children, not us. It isn't ours to decide what or how much these young people will do. It is, however, one of our tasks as youth workers to support and encourage parents in the difficult task of raising teenagers in a Christlike manner. If we can help build bridges between parents and their teenagers, we'll be providing a great service to both.

As we build bonds of trust, we may be called upon from time to time for input in difficult situations. Even here, the more we empower and involve the young person and the parents in a reconciliation process, the more each will ultimately own the outcome and be motivated to give the process all they've got.

Empowerment and healthy boundaries...

ARE • **to be modeled**—Teenagers may not listen to much of what we say, but they notice what we do. If we lack discipline and accountability in our lives, we shouldn't expect them to respect what we tell them about such matters.

The best method of teaching is modeling. Rather than just telling teenagers what to do, it's far more effective to say, "I struggle with that same issue, and that's why I've put some boundaries around my life—even asking others to hold me accountable (watching too much TV, excessive eating or spending, not getting enough rest or exercise, for example). Do you and your other adult leaders demonstrate healthy boundaries in your lives?

ARE • **an essential part of life**—Most teenagers are trying to rid themselves of boundaries, not get more of them. They tend to define freedom as the absence of rules. But nobody can achieve great things without having boundaries in their lives. Every responsibility has a boundary or restriction tied to it.

I often tell teenagers I know only a few people who manage to live without boundaries. They're the homeless people to whom we minister in Boston. No one tells them when they have to come home. No one tells them they have to go to school or work. They can do whatever they want. They have no responsibilities. But is that really freedom? To achieve anything more requires boundaries.

ARE • **most powerful when initiated by youth**—It's one thing to put boundaries around young people. It's quite another when we can remove their boundaries and they set healthy boundaries for themselves, realizing that the boundaries are necessary for them to flourish and to be protected. This is a display of maturity and evidence of readiness to enter adulthood.

ENDNOTES

1. Common quote, source unknown

Providing Empowerment and Healthy Boundaries

Rate your youth ministry in each of the following areas by circling the appropriate number.

1	2	3	4	5
Most of our focus is on trying to control our teenagers.			We try to give as much responsibility as possible to our teenagers, to prepare them for independence.	

1	2	3	4	5
No amount of rebellion is tolerated from our youth.			We try to understand what is behind rebellious attitudes in our teenagers and deal with that.	

1	2	3	4	5
As adults, we tend to decide consequences when rules are broken.			We try to involve teenagers in the decision-making process when consequences are necessary.	

1	2	3	4	5
Boundaries and expectations are not well-defined in our programs.			Both teenagers and adult leaders have a clear understanding of the boundaries and expectations in our programs.	

1	2	3	4	5
Our adult leaders struggle with healthy boundaries.			Our adult leaders exhibit healthy boundaries in their own lives.	

Total score: _____ (Enter this score in the scoring key on page 132.)

CHAPTER 9:
Advocates

Because I often have felt abandoned, I tend to give up on myself too. Therefore, I need at least one advocate who believes in me so I can be a potential advocate for someone else.

So if you consider me a partner, welcome him as you would welcome me. If he has done you any wrong or owes you anything, charge it to me (Philemon 17-18).

Damion's eighteenth birthday was just around the corner. It would be both the best and the worst day of his life. It was the best because he would finally be free! The state couldn't hold him another day. No more people running his life. No one telling him what to do.

It was the worst because he had no place to go, and there was no longer anybody responsible for him. Damion had been locked up for three years, and the only thing he knew on the streets was trouble. He also was convinced he didn't want to go back to that.

Had you asked Damion what he wanted to do when released, he would have said the same thing as nearly every other young person: "I want to get a job, and I want to go back to school." But now he was becoming increasingly concerned because he didn't have any idea how to make either of those two things happen. He was desperately looking for someone to tell him what to do and to show him how to do it.

We had known Damion for more than two years through our Bible study, and were considering taking him into our home. We were living in a small apartment in our church at the time, not an ideal situation for a troubled teenager, but after much prayer and the blessing and support of our church, we decided to take him in.

On the way home from the detention center, I asked Damion what he wanted to see happen with his life. He reiterated, "I want to get a job, and I want to go back to school."

Not wanting to waste any time, I stopped by McDonald's on the way home so he could fill out a job application. "Hey, anyone can get a job at McDonald's, right? Perhaps he could even start working by the end of the week. And the application was only a half sheet of paper," I reasoned.

I had never realized how intimidating a half sheet of paper could be. The first three questions were "Have you ever been locked up?" "Where did you go to school?" and "What is your job history?" Suddenly the sure bet of landing a job didn't look so promising.

I suggested we begin with the last question first. "Have you ever had a job, Damion?" He said he had worked at another McDonald's for a couple of months before he was arrested. "Good. Write that down. If they call them as a reference, it's been so long since you worked there, I'm sure they won't remember you," I assured him.

The interview with the manager went pretty well. The only thing left was to call Damion's job reference. Apparently someone at the other McDonald's did remember him. The manager came out of the office, threw the application at us, and walked away without saying another word. It was a devastating experience for both of us. And I knew the chances of Damion ever filling out another job application were somewhere between slim and none. Clearly, getting a job wasn't going to be as easy as I had envisioned.

When we got home, I called our pastor and told him what had happened. "Let me talk to some of the elders, and I'll get back to you," he said.

The elders agreed to hire Damion part-time to do some yard work and other small projects around the church. They were pleasantly surprised at how well he did. Our pastor then called a friend of his who had a carpet-laying business and told him about Damion.

"I can always use good help," his friend said. "If you say he's good, I'll give him a shot." Damion began that job and worked forty-five to fifty hours a week for the rest of the summer.

As summer was ending, we began thinking about Damion's need to finish his high school education. We always had assumed that students just showed up on the first day of class and got their schedules. But we soon discovered that schools don't want these kinds of teenagers, and trying to get them registered is a major obstacle. Often nobody even knows what grade they're in, for it's difficult to compile the credits from the various schools they've attended while in and out of jail. Few officials are willing to invest all that work since most teenagers like Damion don't go back to school anyway. It's no wonder the vast majority of teenagers released from lock-up never set foot in school again, regardless of how much they say they want to.

After several weeks of persistent calling and meetings, the school reluctantly agreed to allow Damion to enroll as a junior. The second part of Damion's dream was finally becoming a reality.

Now he would need to quit his full-time job and find something part-time. When we asked him where he would like to apply, he said, "McDonald's. I want to prove I can get that job."

"Oh great," I thought, not sure I was up for another round of humiliation. As he filled out the application again, I only hoped the same manager wouldn't come out to interview him. But as luck would have it, she was the one who came out. I quickly left the table for fear she might recognize me.

But this time, Damion had two positive job references. As before, she went into her office and called them both. This time she came back smiling. "When can you start?" Damion worked there until he graduated from high school and left for college. He even became a manager during his last year there.

I often tell the story of Damion to teenagers in jail, especially when we're talking about what it will take for them to make it "out there." When I'm through, I always ask, "Who do you have to meet you when you get out of here? And don't say your mother, because that didn't work last time."

Almost without exception, there's silence. Nearly every teenager looks down and says, "Nobody." Some even ask, "Can you help me find someone?"

We present the same challenge to people in churches. "Are you willing to be the one who will be there for young people like Damion when they get out?" We can't expect them to make it any other way.

Teenagers like Damion need advocates. The dictionary defines an advocate as "one who stands in to plead the cause of another." That's exactly what Paul did for Onesimus, and it's what every troubled young person needs if he or she is going to make it.

But aren't there already programs set up to help these young people? Sure, there are programs, but young people need caring people, not just programs. As criminologist John J. DiIulio so emphatically states, "Strategically, the key to preventing youth crime and substance abuse among our country's expanding juvenile population is to improve the real, live, day-to-day connections between responsible adults and young people—period...No policy, program or intervention that fails to build meaningful connections between responsible adults and at-risk young people has worked or can." [1]

But do teenagers really want our help? Will they even listen to us? Recently, a major national study revealed that while teenagers go to each other first for advice, they tend not to trust the advice they receive. The youth surveyed said overwhelmingly that they would prefer to go to their parents or other adults first, but they don't feel they have the relationship with them to talk openly about their problems. [2]

What Young People Need in an Advocate

What exactly do young people need in an adult advocate? Just how much time is required? Does it really make a difference? We'll examine several different types of advocacy, each requiring its own level of commitment. But first, let's look at three core qualities that must be present for any advocate to be successful.

SOMEONE WHO BELIEVES IN YOUTH

I already mentioned how insecure I was growing up. But one of the best things I did was spend the summers of my junior high school years living with and working for a friend of my parents. Larry operated several farms in southern Minnesota and was a man I idolized.

One evening when my parents were visiting Larry and his wife, I overheard my mother ask him a question: "How do you think Scott's going to turn out?"

I strained with all my might to hear his reply. I'll never forget what Larry said. "Someday Scott will be the president of General Motors." I don't think I slept all night. I felt so good. It was the first compliment I can remember receiving from anyone outside my family. And the fact that he had said it, not knowing that I was listening, made it even more powerful. Though I always knew my parents believed in me, I needed at least one other adult who believed in me as well. Every kid needs someone like Larry, someone who believes in and takes notice of him or her.

Find something specifically good about each of your young people. Follow each one around until you discover it. Then take every opportunity to tell them how good they are. The words you speak will ring in their ears for years to come.

SOMEONE WHO LETS YOUTH OBSERVE THEM

One of the boys in our home recently asked Hanne a question that seemed to come unexpectedly. "You talk a lot to your children, don't you?"

"Yes, I guess I do. What made you think of that?"

"I don't know. I guess it's just that we never did that in my family. Nobody ever talked to each other. I like it, though. And I want it to be that way when I have a family someday." Sometimes the little things we do make the biggest impact.

We have a tradition in our home. When a boy moves out, each of us expresses what he has meant to us. He then has the opportunity to do the same with us. By the time Jake moved out to attend Bible college, he had lived with us for more than two years. We had our traditional going-away ritual for him.

After we had each said our piece, it was Jake's turn to talk. I wondered what he would say about me. We had been through so much together. Would he mention the breakfast and Bible study times we had shared together weekly before school? Those were always rich times for us both. Or might he recall the youth retreats he used to go on with me? Those times away had really served to deepen our relationship.

When he finally came to me, he thought for a while and said, "Two things really stick out in my mind, Scott. The first is that you wrestled with me. My dad never wrestled with me. But you would wrestle with me. If I ever have kids, I'm going to wrestle with them.

"The second thing was watching you and Hanne's marriage. I never really saw a marriage up close. I guess I never even thought I'd get married 'cause it just didn't make sense to me. But now I want to be married some day, and I want to have a marriage like yours." I never would have guessed those things would be so significant to Jake.

This highlights the importance of Paul's statement to the Thessalonian believers: "We loved you so much that we were delighted to share with you not only the gospel of God *but our lives as well,* because you had become so dear to us" (1 Thessalonians 2:8, author's emphasis).

Teenagers need to see firsthand what living as a Christian looks like. Not only do they need to hear the Gospel, they need to see our lives as well. Thus, powerful ministry happens when we're just hanging out with young people, doing something as seemingly unspiritual as wrestling.

For that reason, ministry also is effective when it's done as a married couple. This models to teenagers something many have never seen, a happy marriage. If you're married, allow young people the privilege of seeing you interact as a married couple. If you're a parent, let them see how you relate to your children as well.

SOMEONE WILLING TO LET YOUTH SEE THEIR STRUGGLES

Being open and vulnerable with teenagers is very important for them, both in your struggles as well as in victories. Don't just tell them about the struggles you overcame twenty years ago. Let them see how you're handling some of your current ones. Why? They need to see how Christians deal with their struggles so when they encounter problems they'll know what to do and not conclude, "I must not be a very good Christian, or I wouldn't be going through this."

Shortly after we had opened our home for troubled teenagers, I was talking to a friend on the phone. He asked me how things were going. "It's a lot tougher than I thought it would be," I confessed. "It's a full-time job with one guy. What's it going to be like when we have a house full?"

No sooner had I gotten the words out of my mouth when I turned around and saw Damion standing in the doorway. He had heard every word. He grabbed what he was looking for and left. But by the look on his face, I knew I had hurt him deeply.

I had to rush off to a conference where I was speaking, so I wasn't able to talk with him then. But all the while I was driving, I kept thinking about how foolish I had been for having said such hurtful words.

Finally, I pulled over along the side of the road to phone Damion. "I'm so sorry for what I said on the telephone, Damion. I didn't mean to be hurtful. I was just having a frustrating day. I couldn't be happier that you're living with us. Will you forgive me?" He said yes.

When Damion moved into our home, he said that there were three things he never said: please, thank you, and I'm sorry. But after that experience, saying the words "I'm sorry" came much easier for him.

Different Types of Advocates

At-risk teenagers need various sorts of advocates. One is no more important than another, but we can all advocate in one way or another. Each person should ask God to specifically direct them in this area. Following are descriptions of four different kinds of advocates.

ADVOCATES FOR YOUTH-FRIENDLY ENVIRONMENTS

As we have already discussed, teenagers can be very intimidating to adults. Youth culture analyst Peter Benson has noted that eight out of ten adults avoid making eye contact with youth when they encounter them in public. [3] While teenagers may appear intimidating to us, in general they're more insecure and intimidated than any other age group in our society. They need us to reach out to them rather than to avoid them.

Is your own church a youth-friendly environment? Do people go out of their way to make young people feel welcome? Is the service constructed with their interests and needs taken into consideration when it comes to music, drama, and preaching, or is it designed exclusively for adults? If not, what things can you do to make your church more youth-friendly?

ADVOCATES FOR JUVENILE JUSTICE

Juvenile crime and delinquency are major concerns of citizens around the world. Scarcely a day passes without a report of some heinous crime being committed by a young person.

Out of frustration and fear, concerned citizens and policy-makers in the United States have responded by beginning to dismantle the entire juvenile court system. The 1960s and '70s offered young lawbreakers a combination of punishment, treatment, and counseling in juvenile facilities to straighten out their lives. [4] By the mid-1990s, however, about one in every four juveniles arrested for a violent crime was being placed in adult prison. [5]

The reasoning behind the current trend of placing teens in adult prisons is understandable, but it looks altogether different when you look closer. Dale, one of our adult volunteer Bible study leaders, explains what happened to him.

"I had always believed that kids who committed crimes should receive the maximum sentence, ideally in adult prison. After all, if they're committing an adult crime, they should be serving adult time.

"But I wasn't prepared for what would happen to me when I went into a juvenile detention center for the first time and sat in on a Bible study. I was hooked right away. I had expected to meet rude and hardened criminals, but they were very polite and appreciative. And I guess, more than anything else, they were just kids, kids who seemed a lot more interested in learning about the Bible than those in the high school Sunday school class I was teaching.

"After I had been going in for several months, I asked one of the staff what had happened to Hector. He had become a real leader in our group and was growing tremendously in his faith. The staff said Hector, who was fifteen years old, came in under the new law in Massachusetts that mandated he be tried as an adult and sentenced to fifteen years in adult prison.

"Suddenly, that just didn't seem right to me. Here was a kid who definitely could have been salvaged. He was doing so well in the structured program he was in. But what chance did he have now? These issues began to look entirely different once I got to know some of the kids beyond just what the newspapers said about them."

There is a crying need today for people who are willing to get involved, not only in ministering to young offenders but in advocating for better juvenile justice laws and policies. Isaiah 1:17 clearly admonishes us to "Learn to do right! Seek justice, encourage the oppressed. Defend the cause of the fatherless, plead the case of the widow."

ADVOCATES WILLING TO INTERSECT WITH TEENAGERS

How can your life intersect the lives of troubled youth? One man in our community was concerned about making his construction company into more of a ministry. So he decided to hire some teens being released from incarceration and going back into his city. Sure, this requires him to spend more time with them than most other employees, but he sees that as a ministry.

One church told me of how they had determined to reach troubled teens in their community. Some youth were being sentenced to community service hours, so the church asked the court if they could be an option for community service. Church members would oversee teenagers in projects such as doing yard work and painting for shut-ins, as well as constructing a handicap ramp at the church.

One of the first things that happened was that a VCR mysteriously disappeared from the room where the young people took their breaks. "Oh no," I thought, "This will put a quick end to their attempts at trying to help these youth." I was pleasantly surprised to learn that it hadn't deterred their efforts at all. They decided to keep going ahead, advocating for troubled teenagers in their community.

One lawyer took on some juvenile court cases *pro bono*. Kevin, the boy described in chapter 1, was one of those cases. Kevin credits this man as the reason he decided to go to law school. "He was the first person who really believed in me. He treated me like a son, and I began to think, 'If he believes I can make it, then maybe I can.' Ever since I was fifteen years old, I've wanted to be a lawyer like him. I want to try to help other kids like he helped me."

ADVOCATES WHO ARE FATHERS AND MOTHERS IN CHRIST

The most intense form of advocacy is that of a father or mother in Christ. Dan, an associate staff member with us, serves as a chaplain in a large juvenile facility. He meets hundreds of new teenagers in the course of a year. How can he possibly be a father to all of them? He can't. His degree of involvement varies with each. But there are some to whom God calls him to be a father. Over the years Dan has spiritually adopted, as he terms it, seven different boys. He takes this quite seriously, treating each as his own son long after they leave the institution.

One day, seventeen-year-old Matt, a boy who had been in and out of the institution many times, came into Dan's office. Matt's heart was heavy. He told Dan that all he had ever really wanted in life was a dad, but he'd never had one. Dan tried to comfort him with words about God being a "Father to the fatherless" and "Even though our mother or father may forsake us, God never will forsake us." None of that seemed to help much. Matt walked out of his office feeling about as down as he had when he came in.

Dan couldn't shake Matt's words and the possibility that God might be wanting him to spiritually adopt Matt as his seventh son. So why was he feeling so hesitant? In more than a decade of institutional ministry, Dan had seen almost everything. He'd never had a problem loving and accepting any kid, regardless of his or her crime. Yet one strange fear Dan had possessed since he was a little boy was a fear of vampires. Even as an adult, he occasionally would have nightmares about them.

That's what made the whole thing with Matt so strange. Matt was locked up for "vampirism." His life had been filled with satanic, ritualistic activities such as sucking the blood from animals after killing them. The thought of it repulsed Dan.

Dan had told Matt about Jesus, and he had been working with him to denounce his past satanic involvement. That was one thing. But to make him his son? He wasn't ready for that. Several more weeks went by. God continued reminding Dan of all the repulsive sins he had been saved from. Finally, more out of a sense of obedience than desire, Dan called Matt into his office.

"Matt, I'd like to be your dad. I'd like you to be my son. Not legally, as in the courts and all, but in a spiritual sense. It's something I take seriously, and I've thought about it a lot. It's a commitment I make for a lifetime. I'd like you to take some time to think about it too. Maybe we can talk about it again in a few days."

A couple of days later, Matt asked to speak with Dan privately. With tears in his eyes, he said, "I feel like God is answering all my prayers. I'd really like it if you would be my dad, Dan." More sentimental feelings eventually followed for Dan, but not until he took that first step of obedience.

Being a father or mother in Christ doesn't have to be that formal. But one thing's for sure: You can't fulfill that role in the lives of hundreds of teenagers. Jesus did it with twelve. Dan's attempting it with seven. If God gives you three or four, that's probably enough. You only need to start with one.

Summary

We've been discussing the need today's youth have for advocates.

Healthy advocates...

ARE NOT • **people who just bail out teenagers**—It's tempting to try to "fix" things for young people, to get them out of the jams they get into. But young people need to face the consequences for the poor choices they make. Rather, healthy advocates help teenagers through the process of dealing with consequences so they can learn from them.

ARE NOT • **people who have all the answers**—Good advocates know that being a good listener is usually more important than giving good advice. Once teenagers know you're really hearing them, they'll often ask for advice. That's the best time to give it, for then it's much more likely to be heeded.

Healthy advocates...

ARE • **effective by their presence alone**—Young people often learn as much by observing us in the normal circumstances of life as they learn by what we tell them. Allow teenagers the privilege of entering into your life at work, at home, and at leisure.

ARE • **people who stick by teenagers**—Sometimes teenagers choose to walk away from healthy relationships during times when they're not doing well. Being around you makes them feel embarrassed or convicted of their sin. In those times, don't try to force the relationship. But work hard to leave the door open so when they are ready, they know they can come back.

ENDNOTES

1. John J. DiIulio, "Preventing Crime, Saving Children: Sticking to the Basics," The Prosecutor (November/December 1997), 14.

2. "National Early Teen Survey" conducted in 1998 by KidsPeace, Inc., of Orefield, Pennsylvania.

3. Peter Benson, President of The Search Institute, has used these statistics in numerous speeches he has given.

4. Ted Gest with Victoria Pope, "Crime Time Bomb," U.S. News and World Report (March 25, 1996), 32.

5. Gordon Witkin, "Tough Love in Colorado." U.S. News and World Report (March 25, 1996), 39.

YOUTH MINISTRY EVALUATION

Providing Healthy Advocates for Young People

Rate your youth ministry in each of the following areas by circling the appropriate number.

1	2	3	4	5
Unfortunately we don't have enough adults for each young person to know someone he or she feels close to.			Each teenager has at least one adult who invests in him or her and knows him or her well.	

1	2	3	4	5
Our program doesn't have a "youth friendly" feel to it.			Our program is very "youth friendly" in the music, attitudes of adult leaders, and topics we discuss.	

1	2	3	4	5
We don't think much about juvenile justice issues when we think of youth ministry.			We try to advocate for youth at all different levels, including the juvenile justice system.	

1	2	3	4	5
Our contact with teenagers happens mostly in formal programs.			As much ministry happens outside formal programs as within them.	

1	2	3	4	5
Teenagers who mess up and leave our program don't generally make their way back again.			Teenagers know they always can come back and be welcomed no matter what they've done.	

Total score: _____ (Enter this score in the scoring key on page 132.)

SCORING KEY
Youth Ministry Evaluations

Add up the total number of points you gave your youth program in the evaluation at the end of each chapter. Enter those numbers in the spaces below. Then refer to the bottom of the page for a summary of your youth program's progress in each individual area.

CHAPTER 3: A Father or Mother in Christ, page 51: _____ points

CHAPTER 4: A Genuine Encounter With Christ, page 67: _____ points

CHAPTER 5: A New Identity in Christ, page 83: _____ points

CHAPTER 6: A Place to Belong, page 94: _____ points

CHAPTER 7: Vision and Dreams, page 104: _____ points

CHAPTER 8: Empowerment and Healthy Boundaries, page 120: _____ points

CHAPTER 9: Healthy Advocates, page 131: _____ points

ASSESSING YOUR PROGRAM

Refer to the guidelines below to assess the strength of your youth ministry program in each of the areas covered in Chapters 3 through 9.

    21 to 25 points — Your program is excellent in this area.

    16 to 20 points — You've done well in this area.

    11 to 15 points — You have some room for improvement.

     6 to 10 points — This is a weak area for your program.

      0 to 5 points — Rethink your program in relationship to this area.

at Risk

Another Perspective: God's Agenda is ME

CHAPTER 10: A Heart Exposed

It was July 4, 1991. We had just experienced the biggest miracle of our lives, the fulfillment of a dream. Or was it the beginning of a nightmare? That was the day we moved into a 6,000-square-foot, eight-bedroom house. Not just a nice house, this was to be a discipleship home. It was for boys who made a commitment to Christ through one of our Bible studies while locked up and didn't want to return to their former lives.

God had worked so many miracles to make this day possible. We had no money, yet we were moving into a mansion big enough to comfortably house ourselves, staff members, and up to seven teenagers! We woke up that morning, and our faith was soaring. But by the time we went to bed that night, we were crying. "Oh God, what have we gotten ourselves into?"

Earlier that evening the police had picked up our first boy for jumping over our back fence. When he tried to explain that he lived there, the officer didn't believe him. "Yeah, right. What's a kid like you doing in this neighborhood anyway?" This incident was but a foreshadow of things to come. The only encouragement we could muster up that night was the strong assurance that God had placed us in this home. We knew we were where God wanted us.

Painful Lessons

That first year of operating a home for juvenile delinquents made one reality painfully clear: God's primary agenda was to change *us* much more than the teenagers we would take in. It's amazing how composed you can be in most situations in life, so much so that you begin to feel you've pretty much arrived. Oh, you know you're not perfect, but you're getting close. Well, that first year brought out the worst in both of us. Had we not had four years of a solid marriage and a combined fifty years of faith in Jesus, we wonder if we would have survived with our lives and marriage intact.

Teenagers have a way of exposing the worst in us. Troubled youth don't leave a single stone unturned. Often when God asks us to take a step of faith, God's lessons and agenda first are directed at us. God exposed a number of serious flaws in us during those first few years in that home. Those flaws may not have been so clearly brought to light had we not been in a ministry like this. But they were deadly flaws nonetheless.

As we reveal some of our flaws, you may recognize your own tendency toward some of these destructive ways of thinking. Then you can determine a course of action to correct them.

OBSESSION WITH OUR GOOD REPUTATION

You're never aware of just how committed you are to protecting your reputation until somebody tries to destroy it. Whatever good reputation we had built quickly eroded the moment we moved into that house.

Within a week of settling in, the missions committee chairman of the only church that supported the home took Damion backpacking for the weekend. Everything seemed to go well until a month later when this chairman received his phone bill. It contained over $400 in charges for "1-900" sex calls made the evening Damion spent with him. He was furious and rightfully so. To make matters worse, out of his frustration he made copies of the phone bill to show others in the church. It seemed we were about to lose the only financially supporting church we had, as well as any future invitations to speak there.

Before we had a chance to catch our breath, we saw a notice in our own church's newsletter: "If anyone has any idea who might have made $300 worth of '1-900' calls on the church's telephone, please contact the office immediately." We were embarrassed to have to admit that we might have an idea where the calls came from.

Fortunately, both of those churches still support us, but only because we were able to work with them and with Damion toward a positive resolution, including restitution by Damion. Much to their credit, both churches played a significant role in Damion's life for as long as he was with us.

Later that summer, we took our youth and a group of other teenagers on an overseas mission trip. Again, by all appearances it was a great trip—until two months after the fact, when we received notice that we were being sued by the parents of one of the girls who had been on the trip. Apparently she and one of our boys had rendezvoused, and she was pregnant.

Fortunately, the pregnancy scare turned out to be a false alarm, and the lawsuit was promptly dropped. But meanwhile our reputation was sinking deeper and deeper into the mud. We desperately needed these youth to perform so people would see us as "successful." But the opposite was happening. And we were feeling like failures.

About that time, we attended a prison worker's conference where prison evangelist Frank Costantino was speaking. During his message, he asked how many of us had ever felt like we had failed with a person we were ministering to. I'm sure our hands went up ahead of any others in the room. Then he said, "If you take the blame when someone doesn't turn out well, you'll also be the first to take the credit when they do." Bingo. That was us.

God used these events to whittle away at our need to protect our own good reputation, to be "successful" in the eyes of others. We were beginning to understand why God needed to break us in that area. But it sure was painful.

OUR IDENTITY IN OUR MINISTRY

By the end of that first year, we had burned up four house parent staff members. Each had moved in with a strong sense of feeling called to help us in this new ministry, but all moved out feeling disillusioned. We were beginning to seriously wonder as well if this type of ministry could really work.

And I was beginning to slip into what would be one of the lowest points of my life. Before we had launched this ministry, I had traveled as a youth evangelist, speaking to thousands with an apparent degree of success. Even in the earlier days of this ministry, God's hand of blessing had been obvious. In only a few short years, we had begun Bible studies in nearly every juvenile jail in New England. But now with the opening of this home, I was devoting all my energy to just a handful of teenagers, and from all appearances, they seemed only to be getting worse.

A deep anger was taking root in my life. It was clear to me that I was failing miserably in this ministry of parenting troubled teenagers. Yet I felt trapped. I knew God had placed us there, so there was no other place to turn. But why was God doing this to me? It felt as though God had tricked me into moving into this house only to destroy me.

I recall one time when I harbored so much hatred and anger toward one of the boys that I couldn't even attend our evening devotions. I couldn't bear to sit in the same room with him. So night after night, I would go to our bedroom during that time. Once he even came upstairs and asked, "What's wrong, Scott?" but I couldn't tell him.

At the same time, our marriage was becoming polarized as well. I wanted to kick teenagers out. Hanne wanted them to stay. After a while we couldn't discuss anything pertaining to the home without the discussion becoming a major battle. We both felt alone at a time when we needed each other more than ever because nobody else really understood what we were going through.

We would later resolve never to allow anything to polarize us like that again. It was a lesson we learned the hard way.

Why was this such a difficult time for us? We were beginning to realize just how much of our identity was wrapped up in our ministry. People knew us because of what we did. We were respected because of our ministry. Apart from what we did, we were nothing—at least that's how we felt. Oh sure, we knew such a statement was theologically wrong. I'm sure I had preached more than one message on that very issue. But still that was how we felt.

During those years, I remember thinking a lot about John the Baptist. His earthly ministry was so short. And when Jesus came on the scene, his disciples weren't eager to give up the success they were experiencing. They said to John, "The one you testified about—well, he is baptizing, and everyone is going to him" (John 3:26b).

But what a remarkable man John was. He said, "He must become greater; I must become less" (John 3:30). After perhaps only a couple of months, John the Baptist's public ministry was over.

Could I step aside like that? Was I willing to do whatever God asked me to do even if it wasn't what I wanted? even if it bore little fruit in my eyes? even if it brought out the worst in me? Was I willing for my identity to be swallowed up in God alone? The answers were painfully revealing.

MISUNDERSTANDING SIGNIFICANCE

During this difficult period, I blocked out large amounts of time with the Lord, just to read and pray. I also started meeting with an older friend and mentor to talk through some of the things I was feeling and experiencing. Hanne graciously supported me during that time, encouraging me even when it seemed as though there was no progress being made. But in time, God used all these things to bring me out of my desert.

Part of what I learned about myself was that my dominant need in life is to make a lasting, significant difference. That's why I left a successful career as a stockbroker to go to seminary. It's why I chose to go into youth ministry full time. It's why I believed that opening a home for juvenile offenders was a worthwhile sacrifice.

While that's a noble desire, I had a faulty understanding of where my ultimate sense of significance comes from. That can only be found in Jesus. Graciously, God grants us significant and worthwhile things to do in this life, but our deepest needs for significance will never be met in those things. Only God can meet that need.

The lights went on for me one day when I realized that a handful of juvenile delinquents had the power to control whether I felt my life was worthwhile or not. By their actions, or lack of them, these teenagers controlled whether or not I felt significant, whether or not I felt I was making a lasting difference. It was a recipe for disaster. No wonder I had so much anger and hatred toward them. I had entrusted them with a responsibility only God could handle.

TAKING THEIR PAIN UPON OURSELVES

Nothing burns out a person faster than becoming consumed with another's pain. When the Apostle Paul recounted his list of sufferings in 2 Corinthians 11:23-28—imprisonment, floggings, beatings, stonings, abandonment, days and nights in the open sea, hunger, and nakedness—the list culminated with this: "Besides everything else, I face daily the pressure of my concern for all the churches."

This word translated "pressure" is the same one used earlier where Paul wrote, "We were under great pressure, far beyond our ability to endure, so that we despaired even of life. Indeed, in our hearts we felt the sentence of death" (2 Corinthians 1: 8-9a).

Concern for those we love and those we're called to serve places enormous pressure on us. We were living under that kind of pressure twenty-four hours a day. Because we loved those teenagers, their pain was becoming our pain. And not surprisingly, our reservoirs for helping them were drying up. We had to learn to not make their pain and problems ours but instead to entrust them to God.

So many of our flaws were exposed in those first few years living with teenagers. And although having our weaknesses exposed is never pleasant, God doesn't do it just to make us feel uncomfortable or condemned. God has something far greater in mind—to refine us like gold to make us even more valuable in his service.

CHAPTER 11:
Another Way to Measure Success

A new day dawned for me when I stopped trying to figure out how I could get out of the home we were running. Instead, I began praying, "Lord, please use this home to change me. It's obvious that I'm in need of changing. I've never seen that so clearly as I do now. And I'm convinced that you've placed me here to do a deeper work in me than might otherwise have been possible. I won't leave here until you're finished or until you tell me to go."

Now I was in a position where I could embrace, rather than fight, what God wanted to do in me. Not only could he better work through me to reach others, but I also could find more joy and fulfillment in doing that work. But I had grown accustomed to such a different paradigm of ministry that some other major shifts were needed as well.

The Need for Shift

Though it's important to gauge whether we're being successful in our work, what I really needed was a new way to measure that success. I always had defined success by whether the teenagers I was working with were changing for the better. This definition has at least two inherent flaws, however. The first is that it assumes we somehow have the power to change young people. The second lies in the assumption that we can determine when and if real change has happened in a young person.

Since we're powerless to change young people, we needed to begin to shift some of our focus off them and onto us. We couldn't measure our success by whether teenagers "turned out," but we could measure our success by how we responded to youth. Doing this, however, required at least two major shifts in our thinking. [1]

A SHIFT IN THE SOURCE OF OUR STRENGTH

Most of us really do depend very heavily upon ourselves and others to satisfy our deepest desires. Consequently those relationships are where we get our deepest needs met, rather than through Christ. This is particularly dangerous when it comes to working with troubled young people. When we need them to succeed, we're always in dangerous waters.

JAKE

Jake had come to our house at just the right time. Just when we were wondering if these kinds of teenagers could change, Jake moved in with us. He showed more promise than most teens we had met. A natural leader, Jake had the ability to motivate for good whomever he was around.

While he lived in our home, he would take the other guys to four different youth groups each week, and none of them ever complained about going! Jake just had a way of quietly guiding people toward the Lord.

He played on the varsity football team, and he often would have many of the players over to our house to play pool and hang out rather than getting high or drunk after the games. He would invite them to attend the youth group at our home, and several came. People throughout our community began to know and respect Jake and his faith. He was our pride and joy.

Jake also was the first young person to leave our home and go on to Bible college. And there, too, he flourished. He began taking other students with him into the housing projects to share their faith with the people there. Not only were the people in the projects touched, but his fellow students were profoundly affected as well.

Then we received a phone call from Jake toward the end of his freshman year. After one of the chapel services, he had felt convicted to "come clean" in every area of his life and requested an appointment with the dean of students. He had confessed that he and one of the girls on campus had had sex together early in the school year. He assured the dean that it was no longer happening, that both had repented, and that the incident was well behind them. Jake felt he needed to tell the dean as an act of obedience to the Lord.

In our home, we always had encouraged such openness, rarely giving out consequences to anyone who confessed something completely on their own. The college handled it quite differently. They kicked him out.

Jake was devastated. We told him over the phone that he could come back to the house and live with us until he figured out what should come next in his life. He indicated he probably would, but he was going to his mother's house first.

Jake never did move back into our home, but instead he kept falling deeper and deeper into his former lifestyle—drugs, crime, having children out of wedlock, and going in and out of jail. We tried several times to rescue Jake from that environment, but to no avail.

A disturbing thing was happening inside me at the same time. My concern for Jake was turning to anger. I had invested everything I had into this kid, and still it wasn't enough. He still didn't make it. And I began to resent him for it. He represented for me the fact that my best wasn't good enough.

Tragically, for a long time I wasn't able to invest in another young person to the same extent that I had invested in Jake. I was protecting myself from the potential hurt teenagers could inflict upon me if they were to fall away as Jake had.

This attitude of self-protection caused me to become cynical toward other youth as well. I quit believing in them. That way if they messed up, it wouldn't hurt me so badly because I hadn't invested so much in them anyway. The amazing thing was that many other young people came and went through our home during that time. And many of them did go on to Bible college and succeed there almost in spite of me.

Several times Hanne confronted me on my underlying negative attitude. I would say, "I just don't have that same depth of love to give anymore. I spent it all on Jake." It wasn't that I neglected the youth; I just didn't have the extra amount of energy and emotion I had possessed before Jake came along. I often felt guilty about it, but I felt powerless to change it.

A DIFFERENT KIND OF LOVE

Gradually, God began to reveal to me that what I had termed "love" was very different from the kind spoken about in the Bible. Mine wasn't altogether bad. In fact, it was the best I could offer. It was just woefully inadequate.

I began thinking about how God never withholds love and blessing from us, even though he knows the future and the fact that we may fail miserably and disgrace his name. That blew me away. I always had been willing to invest in any young person, as long as he or she proved to be a worthwhile investment. But when it looked like someone might be going down the drain, I quickly would cut my emotional ties to them, assuring that I wouldn't go down with them.

I began thinking about the way Jesus loved Judas Iscariot. Though he knew Judas would betray him, Jesus never withheld his love from him. He even allowed Judas to be treasurer! I never would have done that. Would you? John 13 beautifully illustrates how Jesus showed Judas the fullest extent of his love, even moments before he would betray him.

I knew I didn't have an ounce of that kind of love in me. But I also was convinced that anything short of it wasn't really love at all. It was merely making a wise investment of my time and energies by loving those who could appropriately reciprocate. Jesus said, "Do not even pagans do that?" (Matthew 5:47b).

I also knew I didn't want to go back to loving the way I had loved Jake in the earlier days. For that wasn't real love either. I was just more naive then. Yet I didn't know enough about this other kind of love to begin applying it.

I began asking God, "How do you handle rebellious kids?" And then more pertinently, "How do you handle me? What keeps you from just giving up?"

I found myself once again drawn to the story of the prodigal son. I had always felt a little uncomfortable with that story. It didn't seem like very responsible parenting to me. After all, how was this kid to learn his lesson, if his father so easily took him back? I had always read this parable through the eyes of the self-righteous older brother. But this time I saw myself not as the older brother, but as the younger one. And for the first time, I was feeling grateful for the father's response.

I also reread the parable of the workers in the vineyard in Matthew 20:1-16. I had never liked that story either. It didn't seem fair that the ones who came to work at six o'clock in the morning were paid the same as those who showed up an hour before quitting time. But for the first time, I realized that I wasn't one of those employees who had shown up at the first hour. I was one of the last-minute employees. In my broken state, that parable took on an entirely different meaning for me. I was the one in need of grace.

And I knew that if I so desperately needed grace, how much more did the young people I was working with need it. I also knew they needed to receive it from me. But where would it come from? I didn't seem to have any to give.

GRACE

Part of my problem was an inadequate definition of grace. I had always seen gracious people as nice, cordial, and not easily prone to anger. But the Bible defines *charis,* the Greek word for "grace," altogether differently. It's "the divine influence upon the heart, and its reflection in the life." [2]

Grace is completely unhuman! It's a God thing. Thus, the only time grace will ever be displayed in our lives is when it's adequately reflected from God himself. Unfortunately, I'm not a particularly good reflector. I've found that I need to receive about a bucketful of grace to dispense a teaspoon to somebody else. But I'm convinced it's been those occasional teaspoons dispensed over the years that have made the real difference in the lives of other people.

Thus, it was becoming increasingly clear to me that I needed to completely shift the source of my strength to effectively minister to hurting teens. I couldn't depend upon my own ability to love them. I just didn't have the kind of love in me that they needed. I had to receive that directly from God. And I had to receive enough so there could be an overflow from me into the lives of the teenagers I had been called to minister to.

A SHIFT IN OUR DESIRES

A second shift that had to take place in me was a shift in my desires for the teenagers with whom I was working. Naturally, I wanted to see their conduct change. But was that God's greatest desire for them?

ONE PARENT'S LESSON

One morning a pastor I know received a disturbing phone call from his wife. She had just discovered that their sixteen-year-old son Danny had come home drunk the night before. It was the first time anything like this had happened with him, and they were both more than a little upset.

The father immediately got in his car and raced home. "How could this have happened?" he wondered. "How could he do this to us?" Danny always had been such a leader in the church and in the youth group. He himself had warned his friends about how to avoid such traps. And now he had fallen into the same thing he was telling them to avoid. What a hypocrite!

And then there was the potential embarrassment this could bring upon him as a pastor and respected leader in the community. People would wonder how he could handle the affairs of the church if he couldn't even manage the affairs of his own family!

The more he pondered, the angrier he became. It was a good thing he had a long drive home. For after venting his frustrations, he finally was able to commit the matter to prayer. As he did, he began to sense God speaking to his heart. "What is your greatest desire for your son? Is it simply that he never drink again? If so, then deal harshly with his behavior, and hope that he won't dare do it again. Or is it your greatest desire that he learn to grow in the grace and knowledge of the Lord Jesus Christ? If that's your goal, then you need to handle it quite differently."

By the time he got home, Danny was waiting. Nervous and shaking, he didn't dare look into his father's eyes. "Son," his father began, "Son, I really love you. I hate what you did. But I want you to know how much I love you."

Before he could go any further, his son broke down and began crying. "Oh, dad. I've heard you say that a hundred times. But now I know it's true. I'm sorry. I'm so sorry. I don't ever want to do that again."

God's will prevailed that day as a father shifted the direction of his desires from simply seeing his son's behavior change to seeing his son grow in the grace and knowledge of the Lord Jesus Christ.

JAKE

By God's grace, I've been able to experience some of that shift as well. More recently, I've been in close contact with Jake again. After he was released from prison, he expressed a desire to get married to the girl he had been living with. He said he wanted to make things right. I performed their wedding.

He also asked me if I would help hold him accountable. "I know I can snow too many people. I need someone who really knows me and isn't afraid to get in my face."

Hanne and I also helped them get an apartment in our community and get jobs and a car. They also have asked us to meet on a regular basis to talk about how to raise their two little girls in a Christlike home.

Jake's story isn't over by any means. The last chapter is yet to be written, and we have no idea how it will end. Their lives go up and down on an almost weekly basis. Some weeks are exciting. Others are very discouraging. But rather than responding to the tumultuous waves they experience, I'm working on loving them more consistently, dispensing God's grace, and praying hard that they'll continue to grow in the grace and knowledge of the Lord Jesus Christ.

A High Calling

I remember praying several years ago, "God, conform me into the image of your Son." Perhaps more than anything else, God has used troubled teenagers to answer that prayer. For certainly I'm not the same person I was ten years ago. I am not even the same as a year ago.

If God has called you to minister to hurting young people, you've been granted a high calling. For not only will the lives of troubled teens be touched, but yours certainly will be changed as well.

As you dare to become involved in the lives of hurting young people, you'll also come to know yourself in a way that might otherwise have been impossible. But beyond that, you'll come to know better the heart and ways of God, and in the process be further conformed to the image of Jesus. What a calling indeed!

ENDNOTES

1. The two following categories were inspired by a section in Kevin Huggins' book *Parenting Adolescents* (Colorado Springs, CO: NavPress, 1989), 151.

2. James Strong, "Greek Dictionary of the New Testament," *Strong's Exhaustive Concordance* (Gordonsville, TN: Dugan Publishers, Inc.), 77.